"Pope Francis's recent text, *The Joy of Love*, is one of the most significant and inspirational church documents ever published on marriage and family. Yet reading such documents can often be a daunting prospect for ordinary Catholics. Julie Hanlon Rubio provides an immensely helpful 'readers guide' to assist ordinary Catholics in recognizing the pope's many remarkable insights on marriage and family life. Her extensive theological background, and engaging writing style, coupled with the helpful discussion questions/suggestions for prayer, make this an excellent resource for the training of those engaged in pastoral care to families/married couples, and a wide range of parish discussion groups."

—Richard Gaillardetz is the Joseph Professor of
Catholic Systematic Theology at Boston College

"In *Reading, Praying, Living Pope Francis's The Joy of Love*, Dr. Julie Hanlon Rubio walks readers through *Amoris Laetitia*. Like an excellent tour guide, she points out what is important about this apostolic exhortation by providing the history behind it and the relevance of it for people's lives today. The result of following Dr. Rubio through the text is a rich appreciation of the pope's vision of love in the family. It is a journey I would highly recommend for everyone."

—Jason King
Professor and Chair of Theology, Saint Vincent College
Editor, *The Journal of Moral Theology*

Reading, Praying, Living Pope Francis's The Joy of Love

A Faith Formation Guide

Julie Hanlon Rubio

LITURGICAL PRESS
Collegeville, Minnesota

www.litpress.org

1	2	3	4	5	6	7	8	9

Library of Congress Cataloging-in-Publication Data

Names: Rubio, Julie Hanlon, author.
Title: Reading, praying, living Pope Francis's The joy of love : a faith
   formation guide / Julie Hanlon Rubio.
Description: Collegeville, Minnesota : Liturgical Press, 2017. | Includes
   bibliographical references.
Identifiers: LCCN 2016037286 (print) | LCCN 2016040110 (ebook) |
   ISBN 9780814645550 | ISBN 9780814645802 (ebook)
Subjects: LCSH: Catholic Church. Pope (2013– : Francis) Amoris lætitia.
   | Families—Religious aspects—Catholic Church—Papal documents.
   | Families—Religious life—Papal documents. | Church work with
   families—Catholic Church—Papal documents. | Marriage—Catholic
   Church—Papal documents. | Pastoral theology—Catholic Church—
   Papal documents. | Catholic Church—Doctrines—Papal documents. |
   Apostolic exhortations (Papal letters)
Classification: LCC BX2351.C2963 R82 2017 (print) | LCC
   BX2351.C2963 (ebook) | DDC 261.8/358088282—dc23
LC record available at https://lccn.loc.gov/2016037286

Contents

Introduction

Front Story and Back Story

Though it has been the subject of no small amount of controversy among church leaders and theologians since its release in spring 2016, the most important thing to know about *Amoris Laetitia* (The Joy of Love) is that it is a letter written by Pope Francis to give hope to Christian married couples. Generally, papal documents have a reputation for being a little on the dry side, but Pope Francis's trademark down-to-earth style comes through in this letter, especially when he addresses married people directly. This guide will walk you through the "back story"—the theological controversies, so that you will understand why theologian fans celebrate the mercy and compassion permeating this letter, while theologian critics worry that it fails to assert Catholic moral norms in strong enough terms. But it will also highlight the "front story"—the core message the pope wants to pass on to Christians around the world, with the hope that they will reflect on it and let it shape their lives.

So, first, some back story. In 2014, Pope Francis stunned the world by calling a synod on the family. The instrument of the synod was created by Pope Paul VI near the close of Vatican II (the historic council of bishops that met in Rome from 1962 to 1965) to provide a formal mechanism by which future popes could continue to consult the world's bishops on pressing issues. Since 1965 there have been approximately fifteen general synods. The pope sets the agenda for the synods and selects bishops from around the world to advise him. This time, bishops gathered in Rome in the fall of 2014 and again in 2015 to discuss how the church could better speak and minister to modern families.

Before the bishops descended upon Rome, they were directed by the Vatican to survey people in their dioceses.[1] One might think that surveying Catholics is unnecessary. After all, if Catholic teaching is not going to change, what is the point of asking people what they think about it? But bishops around the world were told to ask people what they knew about Catholic teaching, what they thought about it, and what they wanted from the church. Though some of the questions provided by the Vatican were weighed down by technical theological language, many were well designed to reach out to a diverse group of Catholic laypeople, many of whom feel alienated or abandoned. Many bishops adapted these questions for use in electronic and paper surveys or focus groups in their dioceses. Catholics interviewed in the media were almost uniformly positive in their reaction to the survey, stressing that whether official teachings changed or not, they were happy that someone noticed existing dissonance, spoke frankly about it, and asked for their opinions about how to move forward.

In the summer of 2014, results were sent to Rome, and bishops who met in working groups on various topics studied the surveys. Along with the expected disconnect (with some variety by region) on Catholic teachings on issues such as contraception, premarital sex, cohabitation, divorce, and same-sex marriage, they found a lack of understanding of the rationale behind those teachings, a need for better pastoral care for families, and a desire to make parishes more welcoming—even for those who may be at odds with official Catholic teaching on sex and marriage. Though a strong level of disagreement on moral norms was undeniable, it seemed that the most urgent requests from the pews were for a new tone, more mercy and compassion, and better pastoral support.

The working documents produced by the synods in 2014 and 2015 showed that the bishops heard Catholics speaking about their hopes and desires for the church. Though some feared the questionnaires would be ignored, the preparatory and final documents produced by the 2014 and 2015 synods all suggest that the bishops of the world were listening to lay Catholics and talking about how best to respond. For example, the 2014 preparatory document notes that parents are "distressed" when their children can receive sacraments but they, due to their "irregular" situation, cannot, and acknowledges that many faithful Catholics do not see a significant difference between contraception and natural family planning.[2] All synod reports make frequent use of the word "accompaniment" to describe how the church should walk with, listen to, and respect people, a hallmark of Pope Francis's preaching and teaching to which people all over the world are responding with enthusiasm.

> The most urgent requests from the pews were for a new tone, more mercy and compassion, and better pastoral support.

The synod documents also made advances in using more "down-to-earth" language to describe marriage. The 2014 preparatory document acknowledged the limits of natural law language that is more typically used in Catholic teaching and articulated a need to move beyond abstract sacramental terms that most Catholics find to be a less-than-perfect lens through which to see their own marriages, though it offered only brief glimpses of what might replace this. In the 2014 midterm report, more relatable language *was* used, even to describe the relationships of same-sex partners who "practice mutual, self-sacrificial love that is worthy of admiration," though this language was subsequently withdrawn in favor of more guarded words about "receiving" those with "homosexual tendencies . . . with respect and sensitivity."[3]

Despite its limitations, the synod on the family was a watershed moment for Catholics. Many felt more welcomed, respected, and understood. They responded to the offers of mercy and inclusion. It seemed that church leaders were following Pope Francis's lead, trying to see "the good amid the weeds" in people's lives and desiring to "throw the doors of the church wide open."[4] Yet, the synod documents have no real authority in the life of the church. They are part of the ongoing Catholic conversation on marriage and family, but it is up to the pope to take the insights of the synod and bring them into the realm of official Catholic teaching.

Thus, it was important that, at the close of the synod, Pope Francis chose to issue his own document, *Amoris Laetitia* (The Joy of Love, hereafter "AL"). This document is an apostolic exhortation (like Francis's *Evangelii Gaudium*, The Joy of the Gospel) rather than an encyclical (like *Laudato Sì*, On Care for Our Common Home). Generally speaking, encyclicals have a wider intended audience ("all people of goodwill") and higher authority than exhortations, which are primarily directed to Catholics. Still, all official papal documents contain various levels of Catholic teaching, from observations about cultural change, to moral exhortation, to expressions of long-standing Catholic doctrine. Catholics are committed to approaching this whole body of work with respect and a desire to be better formed as disciples of Christ. Since the last papal encyclical on marriage (*Casti Connubii*, On Christian Marriage) was issued in 1930, it seems safe to say that AL should be regarded as the most up-to-date synthesis of authoritative Catholic teaching on marriage and family, and the best source for today's Catholics seeking inspiration on how to live up to the demands of Catholic, sacramental marriage.

Reading a papal document can be like reading a catechism, a theology book, a spirituality guide, or a committee document all at once. Some passages explain Catholic teaching in a very basic way. Others are more speculative, as the pope makes an argument by, for instance, applying an old concept to a new problem, drawing on secular sciences to understand new phenomena, or employing poetry in order to get at the depth of a human reality that religious people have been trying to understand forever. Some passages are genuinely beautiful, and could be inspirations for prayer or pondering. Others are quite technical, and seem to be there in order to satisfy the concerns of particular influential groups. Especially in AL, the pope often quotes from the synod documents I discussed above or speaks to the concerns of different factions of bishops who argued behind closed doors during the synods. During the synods, he encouraged frank discussion and called the bishops to keep talking through their disagreements.[5] In AL his goal is to show that while the concerns of all were heard, the church must choose a way forward, and that way is one of welcome, accompaniment, and mercy. Still, Pope Francis chooses a way that opens doors rather than closes them.

The very beginning of the document reveals the pope's concerns. A contrast with Pope John Paul II's 1981 apostolic exhortation, *Familiaris Consortio* (On the Family [FC]), also written after a synod on the family, is helpful.[6] Unlike John Paul II, who addresses himself to bishops, clergy, and "the faithful," Pope Francis notes that he writes especially to "Christian married couples." Instead of addressing a broad social problem ("the role of the Christian family in the modern world"), he identifies an opportunity to speak "on love in the family." Rather than beginning with the idea that the family is in crisis (FC 1), Francis opens with the common

> The church must choose a way forward, and that way is one of welcome, accompaniment, and mercy.

experience of the joy of love (AL 1). He remembers the synod as a vibrant "process" involving learning, debate, and discussion (AL 2), thereby giving his official blessing to ongoing, lively conversation within the church. Finally, he chooses not to invoke his authority to settle all the controversies that arose during the synod. On the contrary, he asserts that he will not try to answer all questions, but will share with married couples the wisdom of the tradition as it relates to contemporary realities, while accepting a certain level of diversity among Catholics (AL 3).

The "back story" to the introduction to AL includes all that the bishops learned from the pre-synod surveys: the church's failure to communicate essential wisdom about marriage in terms ordinary people would understand and find inspiring, an excess of judgment that drives people away, a too-narrow focus on moral claims that are no longer credible, a longing for a church that respects and walks with people. With all of this in mind, Pope Francis announces a new tone and a substantive shift from controversial rules to the positive aspects of what it means to live and love in a Christian family. This becomes the "front story" of his document on marriage.

This guide is designed to help you work through AL by providing necessary context (or "back story"), highlighting key points ("front story"), suggesting directions for prayer, and providing questions about how to live out the Christian vision of marriage and family. It assumes no background knowledge and can be used by individuals, groups, or classes. As you go, it will be helpful to keep the following key themes in mind. Though not addressed chronologically, they come up repeatedly and constitute the "take-away" of the document. Look for them as you read and note how they provide the scaffolding on which the rest of the exhortation is built.

1. *Intimacy and passion are good in themselves and worth cultivating for life.* Let no one say that for Catholics sex and

marriage are only for procreation. Pope Francis spends most of his time and energy talking about love, intimacy, and passion. The Christian tradition has many thinkers who had a hard time seeing this core of marriage. Saint Augustine, for instance, famously identified the three goods of marriage as offspring, (sexual) fidelity, and the sacramental bond that tied spouses to each other for life. Love did not make the list, and sex was at best a necessary evil that kept spouses from the greater evils of promiscuity and might, if they were lucky, produce children who would grow up to become vowed celibates. Francis improves upon this tradition by focusing on a passionate love that is deserving of attention and cultivation for a lifetime.

2. *Christians accompany people who experience brokenness or failure in marriage.* Our role is not to judge but to support. We do this individually and as a church. Francis recognizes that many people are doing the best they can but are often unable to keep their marriages together or treat family members as they deserve to be treated. He urges us to approach failure with mercy and acceptance, and affirms the church's trust in adult Christians who make decisions in good conscience. In providing less judgment and more accompaniment, the church holds on to the demanding ideal but recognizes the frailty of human beings and respects their ability to make their own decisions.

3. *Social forces make marriage difficult to sustain.* The pope thinks about marriage in a global context and takes note of realities that impede the living out of the ideal: poverty, migration, incarceration, racism, exploitation, trafficking, etc. In the United States, sociologists refer to two marriage cultures, distinguishing the well educated and financially comfortable (who marry more often and divorce

less frequently) from the less educated and more financially challenged (who marry less often and divorce more frequently).[7] Marriage is easier to initiate and sustain for those who are more privileged in life. Being "pro-marriage" means caring about social issues, too. In Catholic social thought, as Pope Francis says, "everything is connected," which means that caring about family means caring about the forces that make it difficult for families to thrive.[8]

4. *Married life is imperfect.* Previous Catholic teaching could be alienating when it spoke of married love using words or analogies that seemed totally divorced from real-life relationships. To correct this, Pope Francis identifies common problems that frequently distort married love (i.e., domination, infidelity, abuse, and neglect). Though he repeats traditional claims about married love echoing the trinitarian love of God, he is quick to say that no one married couple ever loves this perfectly, and should not be expected to!

5. *Love is fruitful.* The primary emphasis on intimate love does not rule out a broader conception of love. The claim here isn't simply that an "end" or purpose of sex is procreation (that's the natural law language we're trying to improve upon!) but that married love in its essence points beyond itself to more. If cultural ideals of romance are communicated in stories of young adults who meet and fall for "the one" with whom they want to spend every moment of every day forever, the Christian ideal is more expansive. Love between two people naturally spills over, most often in children, but also in shared projects, a welcoming home, and a life lived together in service to others. For Christians, the point is not to "focus on the family" but to find a spouse to love and to partner with in acting for justice in the world.

These five themes comprise the "front story" of The Joy of Love. Keep them in mind as you read, and remember that they constitute the core of the document, and are much more important than ongoing "back story" battles over rules and norms. To be sure, the document does not ignore rules and norms and I'll draw attention to points where the pope makes normative claims. However, there is much more to the moral life, and to married life in particular, than rules. For instance, knowing Catholic norms on contraception and abortion is important, but that still leaves a lot to be said about what it means to parent well, and most of that cannot be expressed in rules. Similarly, knowing that adultery is immoral is just the beginning of thinking about what it means to be faithful to one's spouse on a daily basis. Most of AL is devoted to ordinary family life and the daily struggle of trying to love family members well. All people who live that life are familiar with its many challenges. If you read AL looking for wisdom for those kinds of challenges, and if you're lucky enough to be reading it with others who bring wisdom born of life experience of their own, you won't be disappointed.

ASSESSING

Where Are We?

How does one begin to talk about family? In most of Catholic social teaching, whether the subject is economics, the environment, or war, writers begin by summarizing, with the help of scholars in the physical and social sciences, what is going on or by describing what is sometimes called "the situation." Theologians, bishops, and popes take on "the responsibility of reading the signs of the times and of interpreting them in the light of the Gospel" (*Gaudium et Spes* 4). In the documents of Catholic social teaching, there is room for the church to learn from the world and develop in its understanding of what it means to be a good person in the world (GS 44). However, in Catholic sexual ethics, whether the subject is contraception, same-sex marriage, or extramarital sex, it is more common for popes to begin by reviewing Catholic teaching, establishing universal principles to be applied to any new situation, and there is less attention to secular movements from which the church may need to learn.

Marriage and family concerns occupy a unique place between social ethics and sexual ethics. Many official documents belonging to the body of Catholic social teaching devote some attention to family, envisioning families as having a crucial role in sustaining good societies. Family is a part of Catholic social teaching.

However, family is also a part of Catholic sexual ethics. If you go to the website of the United States Conference of Catholic Bishops (USCCB), for instance, a list of documents related to marriage and family includes *Humanae Vitae* (1968), the famous encyclical that reaffirmed official Catholic teaching on contraception, along with other documents focusing primarily on sex. As many contemporary scholars have noted, though common values run through all of Catholic moral theology, the method (or approach) can differ depending on whether the issues in question are social or sexual.

So what does Francis do here? Respecting the unique position of family in Catholic thought, he has *two* starting points: the Catholic tradition (chap. 1) and the situation (chap. 2). And, even within these chapters, he moves back and forth between ideal and reality. Instead of choosing to begin *from above* (with the tradition) or *from below* (with the situation), in AL he maintains a dialogical posture that is very much in keeping with his posture as pope. Pope Francis seems to be always out in the world, is willing to talk with anyone, has a special concern for those who have been left out, and consistently focuses on the heart of the gospel message. He is a pope devoted to dialogue. This dialogical starting point, which has allowed Pope Francis to be both approachable and prophetic, is the method and genius of AL.

1 "In the Light of the Word" A Biblical Vision

Begetting and raising children . . . mirrors God's creative work.
—AL 29

Pope Francis opens this section by giving readers a distinctive lens for approaching the Bible. Instead of looking to the Bible for rules about marriage and family (i.e., "What does the Bible say about *x*?"), they should pay attention to the stories and, above all, to the mosaic that is created when we read those stories together. The Bible, he claims, from its first page to its last, "is full of families, births, love stories and family crises" (AL 8). Francis begins with a traditional image from Psalm 128 (a man, his wife who is like "a fruitful vine," and his children who are like "olive shoots" [AL 8]) in order to paint a vibrant picture of a family gathered at table and to establish an anchor for this section. But pay attention to how this image is complicated as the pope weaves the different biblical stories into a colorful tapestry.

Note how he begins by stressing fruitfulness (AL 8, 11, 14). Of course, not all married couples have children. Still, even today, most couples bring children with them into marriage or desire biological or adopted children. However, even in Catholic theology, which requires openness to children for a legitimate marriage, couples who cannot have biological children due to age or infertility are understood to have just as sacramental a marriage as any other couple. *All* married couples are seen as fruitful because their love is not insular; it begins with the two of them and goes beyond them.[1] Just as fecundity or creativity is fundamental to who God is, it is an essential quality of marriage, whether children are involved or not.

Yet, recall that fruitfulness is but one of the five major themes of AL. Passionate, faithful love (theme number one) is given more attention and developed more fully in the document. Remember, in Catholic theology, children are important to marriage, but marriage is not all about children. The passionate love of the spouses for each other constitutes the core of marriage, the essence without which marriage cannot exist. Marriage reflects the reality of God: as God is loving, so too are husbands and wives loving.

Pope Francis links the creation stories of Genesis 1 and 2 with two biblical texts that are much less commonly utilized in papal documents: the Song of Songs, which celebrates passionate sexual love, and Psalm 63, which includes the provocative phrase "My soul clings to you" (AL 12–13). Pope Francis uses these texts to paint a picture of sexual, emotional, and free self-giving in marriage. Unlike many Christian thinkers in the past who were so worried about the potential selfishness of sexual love that they failed to celebrate it, Pope Francis gives eros its due.

> Marriage reflects the reality of God: as God is loving, so too are husbands and wives loving.

Notice how the document then moves to the home, describing it as a place of formation, or, in the words of *Gaudium et Spes*, "a school for human enrichment."[2] Lest this sound like something anyone claiming "traditional values" might say, the pope makes sure to cite the biblical source for this vision of the home: the earliest Christian communities that met not in church buildings, but in the homes of their members (AL 15). Our knowledge of this early tradition is sketchy, but, building on the available sources, we can imagine that when adults (men and women, free and slave) and children left the religions of their families, converted to Christianity, and made the choice to attend Christian rituals, they were making a pretty serious choice, one that sometimes put them at odds with their family members (Matt 10:34-36). And we can also imagine that these rituals of remembrance were formative of the moral commitments of these early Christians, who often embraced radical positions.[3] This is the tradition the pope draws upon in order to make a moral claim about families. Christian homes should be places where character is formed, where adults and children are prepared to take the ethos of the New Testament into the world (AL 16–17).

What is that biblical ethos? Pope Francis does not limit his discussion to "family values," because the biblical ethos is much broader and deeper than this. Instead, as in all of his ethical teaching, the pope focuses on the core message. He lifts up Jesus' selfless love and highlights male and female images of God's tenderness as the cornerstones of a biblical family ethics. He notes that a close reading of Jesus' parables shows a concern with the anxieties and tensions of families (often in the face of sickness, abandonment, or death [AL 21]). Finally, he briefly mentions the parts of the gospel that sit uncomfortably with a focus on family: Jesus' many puzzling sayings that call family ties into question.[4]

How can we hold this radical strain of our tradition together with all the passages that lift up family? The pope suggests that Jesus is pointing us to "other, deeper bonds" (AL 18). Some scholars would want to go further here and claim that Jesus calls his followers to reconsider the prominence of family ties, and place greater hope in the community of Christian believers.[5] At the very least, the biblical ethos of AL includes a recognition that discipleship is the primary call of every Christian and a view of family as one kind of community in which it is possible to live out that call.

Pope Francis helpfully calls attention to the presence of, shall we say, problems in the families portrayed in the Bible. There is no way to talk about "the biblical family" without acknowledging biblical family sins such as adultery, rape, murder, abuse, betrayal, and domination (AL 19–20). Along with these personal sins that cause pain in families, the pope notes that what the Catholic tradition calls structural or social sin (like poverty, unemployment, and environmental destruction) also hurts families (23–26). The biblical vision of the family might begin with the happy parents and loving children, but it does not deny the reality that families are the locus of much pain in life, because of the persistence of personal and social sin.

Pope Francis presents a colorful and complicated mosaic of the biblical family in this first chapter, yet he insists on this analogy: families are "icons" or images of God. If this image still seems overly ideal, the pope asks us to focus on the holy family—not the overly idealized images you might see in art museums, but the reality. When Jesus came into the world, the holy family was a refugee family living in an occupied territory (AL 30). And of course we know that the holy family did not exactly follow the traditional script. Mary found herself pregnant while betrothed, Joseph stood by her but tradition suggests he died before Jesus reached adulthood, Mary spent most of her life as a single mother, and Jesus never married. The Bible, the pope is saying, does not give us an impossible ideal but rather assures us that, whatever our circumstances, the love we share in families can give us the best hints we have on earth of how much God loves every human being.

Families are "icons" or images of God.

Suggestions for Prayer

1. Are there experiences in your own family that could be pondered or taken to heart as Mary pondered her own family situation in light of God's work in her life (AL 30)?

2. Can you imagine Jesus, who spoke in his parables of the anguish of parents, spouses, and siblings, comforting you and others in your family in your struggles (AL 21–22)?

Discussion Questions

1. What structural sins do you see harming families in your community?

2. Does it make sense to think that family life can tell us something about the nature of God? If so, can you think of a particular experience that made this clear to you? Can family life also raise profoundly troubling questions about God?

2 Experiences and Challenges
Family Life Today

We also find it hard to make room for the consciences of the faithful, who very often respond as best they can to the Gospel amid their limitations, and are capable of carrying out their own discernment in complex situations. We have been called to form consciences, not to replace them.
—AL 37

This section, the second part of the introduction to AL, presents the "current reality of the family," which the synod fathers (e.g., the bishops attending the synods) examined via discussion of surveys and their own pastoral experiences. Pope Francis is clear from the outset that in this document, he does not simply intend to say what the church has always said about marriage and family. Rather, he seeks to deepen and broaden the church's understanding of marriage and family by attending to the current situation (AL 31). He is not uncritical of what he sees in the world, but he begins this section with an important passage in which he acknowledges how the church's failures have contributed to present social ills, how impossible it is for the church "to impose rules by sheer authority," and how the church has overemphasized procreation and presented a far too abstract teaching on marriage that has been unattractive to many (36). This self-criticism is striking and uncommon in official Catholic documents, especially those on sexual or family ethics. As you read, think about how Francis is trying to balance the idea that the church can learn from the world with the claim that the church can offer wisdom to the world that transcends the times.

Catholic social documents frequently have a section on "the situation" in which many topics are briefly alluded to but not discussed in depth. This can be frustrating for the reader. I offer as a road map some categories that can help you navigate this material. The pope thinks about the reality of the situation in four keys: ways of thinking, social structures, common stresses, and less-than-ideal forms. In each area, he affirms what is good while calling out problems that make it harder for families to thrive.

Ways of Thinking

The major problematic "way of thinking" identified by the pope is an overly narrow view of freedom. Note how some advances in freedom are lauded (e.g., parents are less authoritarian, spouses are more equal, "authenticity" is preferred to "mere conformity," AL 32, 33). However, the pope worries about "an extreme individualism which weakens family bonds," and "an overly individualistic culture, caught up with possessions and pleasures" (33). He wants to affirm the importance of freedom of choice while making sure that the lives of our choosing are truly good and generous. He is particularly worried about what happens to the exclusivity and stability that are so essential to marriage when we prioritize individual desires (34). Yet he does not want to turn back to a kind of church teaching that emphasized sacrifice, submission, and fidelity to the marriage bond while failing to respect the freedom of conscience of individual

Catholics (37). There must be a version of freedom that makes room for sacrifice.

Other problematic ways of thinking are similarly given nuanced treatment. Just as the pope avoids overly simplistic condemnations of individualism, he worries about "a purely emotional and romantic conception of love" (AL 40) without dismissing the value of passionate connection. In the United States 94 percent of young adults say they want to marry their soul mate, yet social scientists tell us that the important thing is not finding "the one" but being willing to work together through all the joys and challenges life offers.[1] As we saw in chapter 1, the pope affirms the goodness of passionate love, but he shares with many experts on marriage a worry that searching for "the one" leads young adults to marry for the wrong reasons. Moreover, overly romantic conceptions of marriage are linked with disappointment and marital breakup when people decide they have chosen the wrong person. As the world has moved away from institutional marriage to companionate marriage, the church, too, has come to affirm the importance of love at the core of marriage. In this document the pope strikes a balance, affirming passion while remaining skeptical of romanticism.

Note how the critique of problematic ways of thinking about marriage in this section is similar to Pope Francis's critique of consumerism. He sees similarities between a "throwaway," temporary consumer culture in which we buy things only to discard them when new things come along and a temporary marriage culture in which partners are abandoned when they fail to satisfy (AL 39). Although the analogy is somewhat strained, the document asks readers to consider whether the

> There must be a version of freedom that makes room for sacrifice.

> The church has come to affirm the importance of love at the core of marriage.

cultural value on newness and satisfaction could infiltrate our approach to family life. Related concerns include what Francis calls "a mentality against having children" (a priority on maintaining a certain lifestyle that leads couples to postpone or avoid having children, AL 42) and an impoverished sexual ethos driven by an excessive emphasis on sexual pleasure that, again, privileges satisfaction of individual desires over the work of maintaining commitments to lifelong relationships.

Although the pope's comments on gender come later in this section, I would place them under the "problematic ways of thinking" heading. Here it is important to point out that the main problem being addressed is sexism, which is manifest in social customs (e.g., female genital mutilation, polygamy, arranged marriages, young girls forced into marriage) and in the pervasiveness of domestic violence, which "contradicts the very nature of the conjugal union" (AL 54). The absence of fathers, which is epidemic, is also called out (55). Note that the pope makes a stronger claim about violence than he does about any other problem in this section. The prominence given to family violence by Pope Francis is unprecedented in Catholic teaching. Moreover, the pope celebrates "the working of the Spirit" in modern movements for women's rights and the rise of "reciprocity" or mutuality in marriage (54).[2]

However, he also challenges forms of what he calls "an ideology of gender" (a puzzling term) that deny all differences between men and women and view sexual identity as "the choice of the individual, one which can also change over time" (AL 56). It is worth noting that the pope is quoting extensively from the final document of the 2015 synod, respecting the concerns some bishops brought to Rome. He maintains that though sex and gender can be distinguished, they cannot be completely severed. Key to his thinking here is the statement, "We are creatures, and not omnipotent. Creation is prior to us and must be received as a gift" (56). The pope's comments bring to mind recent discussions about transgender persons, and especially views of sexual identity that understand it as something discovered or chosen by each individual.

A thorough discussion of gender is impossible here, but we can acknowledge the following: (1) The science on transgender persons is complicated and evolving. Some individuals are born with ambiguous indicators of sex, making identification of their given sex difficult. So far, there is no official Catholic position on what ought to be done in these cases. (2) Gender theory is complicated and evolving. Most scholars see gender rooted in both biology and culture, but there is a great deal of variation and ongoing discussion. (3) Over time, Catholics have come to see more difference between sex and gender. Some things we think of as feminine or masculine apply to some people more than others and apply in some cultures more than others. Contemporary Catholic teaching has evolved from a hierarchical model to a model stressing equality along with difference as central to marriage. Beyond that, when it comes to gender, there is a lot of disagreement among theologians, scientists, and ordinary Catholics.

Read the pope's comments on sex and gender with this debate in mind and take time to think about where your own views come from and how they have changed over time. Ask about the views of others in your group. Remember, this is complicated stuff! If Christians in the nineteenth century had to grapple with Darwin's theory of evolution and rethink their whole approach to Scripture and creation, today scientific discoveries relating to sex and gender present similar challenges.

Sinful Social Structures

Identifying problematic ways of thinking as threats to marriage is common in Catholic theology. The pope does this, but he also identifies problematic social structures that make marriage more difficult to sustain. AL addresses the following issues: general lack of support (32, 42–43); inadequate housing (44); a lack of recognition of family rights, including the right of adult earners to a family wage (44); a failure to adequately respond to violence against and sexual exploitation of children (45); economic situations that drive people to migration and trafficking, breaking up families and endangering women and children (46); and the failure to support single parents living in poverty (49). The important thing to notice here is that the pope realizes that there are things beyond families' control that make their life difficult, sometimes extraordinarily so. He calls society to own its duties to families and he insists that the church's response when faced with situations like these should be marked by mercy and light (49).

Common Family Stressors

This section shows that the synod fathers listened to what people wrote in surveys about the difficulties they face every day in their families. As you read, you can think about how the struggles they identified match up with those that are prominent in your own context. The bishops named the challenges of caring for children and adults with disabilities (AL 47); caring for elders (48); trying to raise kids well, dealing with the intrusion and distraction of technology and time pressures (50); addiction (51); and violence (51). If church teaching on family has often primarily spoken of the hot-button issues (i.e., contraception, divorce, extramarital sex), this document aims to include other kinds of concerns weighing on the hearts of people who live in families. Pope Francis wants Catholics to know that the bishops heard people asking for understanding and support and that they began talking about how to offer what people actually need.

Problematic Family Structures

There was a lot of debate at the synod about how to approach Catholics living in nontraditional family structures (e.g., prenuptial or nonnuptial cohabitation, same-sex union, polygamy, arranged marriage). The bishops struggled to figure out how to welcome people with mercy while also calling them to the fullness of the Catholic vision of marriage. Francis responds with his own attempt to communicate the depth and beauty of lifelong marriage while not failing "to acknowledge the great variety of family situations that can offer a certain stability" but are not the same as marriage. He says, "No union that is temporary or closed to the transmission of life can ensure the future of society" and calls for efforts to strengthen marriage (AL 52).

He is *not* saying that things were perfect in some prior "golden age," nor is he advocating a return to a traditional family model that he acknowledges was authoritarian, and sometimes violent. Yet, he seeks authentic renewal of marriage and family, not something else altogether (53). To be sure, many theologians, like the majority of US Catholics, would not necessarily place same-sex union on the same list with polygamy and arranged marriages, because they believe same-sex couples can realize the essential goods of marriage: union and fruitfulness. Others wonder if cohabitation could be incorporated as a stage of marriage, or struggle with pastoral questions of how to lead cultures traditionally tied to arranged marriages or polygamy to freely chosen, lifelong companionate marriages.

Vision

This section began with Pope Francis's insistence that the church learns from the world and must respect the consciences of people of faith. Yet, in spite of the worries of some traditionalists, this dialogical starting point did not stop the pope from identifying problems in the world that need to be addressed. According to the pope, those who want to strengthen marriage have a lot of work to do. But Pope Francis is well positioned to engage people in that work because he uses a dialogical model that respects those with whom he converses. He does not fail to admit the church's errors and excesses nor does he fear pointing out the good things present in history and culture. He reaches out to his readers, assuring them he knows that they value lasting marriage (AL 38). He assures them that marriage is not an externally imposed "lifelong burden," but rather, at its best, it can be "a dynamic path to personal development and fulfilment" (37). It is, in fact, what people seek, the answer to their dissatisfaction and loneliness (43).

In the sections to come, the pope will try to present the Catholic vision in a more attractive way. But with this section's foray into the reality of marriage, his readers know that while the pope will present a "demanding ideal," he aims to follow in the footsteps of Jesus, who "never failed to show compassion and closeness to the frailty of individuals" (38). This will be a vision of marriage with a heart.

Suggestions for Prayer

1. Choose one of the problematic ways of thinking identified in the document to meditate on. How might it negatively impact your commitment to family?

2. Think of people you know well who struggle with difficult family situations. Spend time bringing their concerns to prayer. Ask if there is anything you might do to help.

Discussion Questions

1. What has the church learned from contemporary feminism or other movements for gender and sexual equality? What might the church still need to learn?

2. Which of the problematic social structures identified in the document do you see impacting the families around you? Is there anything parishes can do to help?

SEEKING WISDOM

What Is Marriage?

Chapters 3, 4, and 5 are the core of AL, the place where the "front story" about marriage is told. Some commentators even suggest beginning with chapter 4 instead of reading the document from the beginning. Notice that in this "vision" section, the pope draws on two key sources of wisdom: Catholic tradition and married couples. His main contribution in chapter 3 is reading the tradition through the gaze of Christ, or with the essence of Jesus' preaching and the force of his compassion in mind. The pope knows that if he simply repeats the rules, he will fail to inspire. He also knows that the church can learn about marriage from attending to the internal lives of married couples (theme one: passionate love) and to the ways their married love spills over and creates new life (theme five: love is fruitful). His goal in this second part of AL is to construct an attractive vision of marriage from "above" (the tradition) and "below" (people's experiences) that resonates and challenges.

3 Beginning with the Gaze of Christ
Looking Again at Tradition

Our teaching on marriage and the family cannot fail to be inspired and transformed by this message of love and tenderness; otherwise, it becomes nothing more than the defence of a dry and lifeless doctrine.
—AL 59

Weddings are perhaps more popular than ever, but the Catholic vision of marriage is less compelling to many. Bride magazines, reality TV shows devoted to overzealous brides and their bridesmaids, and movies about wedding crashers have never been more popular. We see ever more elaborate proposals, engagement photos, and wedding receptions. At least in the United States, despite what some social commentators predict, there is little danger of marriage fading away. Yet, many have questions about what constitutes the essence of marriage: What if you never meet "the one"? Is it really possible to love someone for a lifetime? What if you fall out of love? Is marriage a sacrament or is it a human institution? How much forgiveness is too much? Why does marriage need to include children? Why can't Catholics be more accepting of diversity? How can a bunch of celibate men claim to teach authoritatively on marriage? In short, there is a lot of suspicion about Catholic views of marriage.

This is why Pope Francis puts a somewhat different spin on what, in many respects, is a familiar summary of the Catholic tradition on marriage. He cites the standard biblical passages. He notes Jesus' rejection of divorce in Matthew 19:3-12, which points back to the creation story of Genesis 2:24 and thus to the idea that human beings are created by God for "one flesh union." He recalls the story of Jesus' first miracle at the wedding of Cana (John 2:1-11). Though this may seem a relatively thin basis for a whole theology of marriage, Catholics have built their understanding of marriage largely on these texts and the famous passage from Ephesians 5:21-32, which the pope also cites. But because the pope correctly perceives that people hearing this "case" often perceive it as "the defense of a dry and lifeless doctrine," he doesn't stop here. He fills out the tradition using depictions of families in Jesus' ministry and parables (such as Jesus' friendship with Lazarus, Martha, and Mary, and his encounters with the Samaritan woman and the woman found in adultery, AL 64).

Remember, the pope approaches Scripture as a narrative that forms the Christian imagination, not a rule book. And by including stories of single-parent families, families dealing with illness and death, and families marked by violence, he hopes to show that Scripture does not present an impossible ideal. Rather, in reading about all of the varied families in Scripture and seeing how Jesus tells their stories and welcomes them in his ministry, Christians can come to see Scripture as a source of hope that every family, no matter how "imperfect," can be "a light in darkness" (AL 66).

The Catholic tradition is not solely based on Scripture. We also affirm the existence of natural law, which means we are convinced that we can use reason to discern true things about who human beings are and how they are meant to live in the world. Though the language of natural law may be difficult today, the concept of gaining wisdom through reason is fundamental to the Catholic tradition and continues to resonate. This is why the pope moves from the Bible to a brief survey of recent magisterial teaching on marriage. But as with any historical survey, the framing is important. Here the pope emphasizes the continuity with which his predecessors (Pope Paul VI, Pope John Paul II, and Pope Benedict XVI) have spoken to the importance of love and intimacy in marriage. (Because for Catholics, marriage is not just about procreation, right?)

> The concept of gaining wisdom through reason is fundamental to the Catholic tradition and continues to resonate.

In emphasizing love, Francis insists, he is not doing something totally new. Even *Humanae Vitae*, the 1968 encyclical known for reaffirming Catholic teaching against contraception, stresses the importance and holiness of intimacy between spouses. Before the Second Vatican Council, the church sometimes gave the impression that religious life was the only *real* vocation, the choice that allowed for the true pursuit of holiness. However, for the last fifty years, marriage has more and more come to be understood as a "vocation" and a "call to holiness" that can be every bit as demanding as life as a priest or nun. Theologian Richard Gaillardetz goes so far as to call marriage "a daring promise," an ascetical vocation requiring conversion, sacrifice, and a willingness to change for the other person.[1] This is the challenging contemporary vision of Catholic marriage.

> Marriage is an ascetical vocation requiring conversion, sacrifice, and a willingness to change for the other person.

The pope also tries to explain what it means to call marriage a sacrament.

Notice that paragraph 71, which repeats Catholic claims from Scripture and uses traditional language, is taken directly from the final document of the synod (AL 71). In paragraphs 72 and 73, Francis tries to make sacramental theology more accessible by weaving together portions of John Paul II's *Familiaris Consortio*, the Catechism, a 2014 synod document, and an earlier sermon of his own. He tries to balance the idea that "mutual belonging" in marriage is a true sign of Christ's love for humanity with the reality that any one married couple can only imperfectly symbolize the all-encompassing love of Christ. The sacrament of marriage is both "a *gift* given for the sanctification and salvation of the spouses" and "a specific *call*" (72, emphasis added). Couples are not alone in their marriage, for Christ "dwells with them, gives them the strength to take up their crosses and so follow him, to rise again after they have fallen, to forgive one another, to bear one another's burdens." Yet because human response and effort are also required, the analogy between marriage and Christ and the church is "imperfect" (73). The sacrament in marriage is both always present and always partial, in process.

A further ambiguity in Catholic teaching is explored in paragraphs 76–79: How can marriage be both natural and supernatural? Francis explains that natural marriage (civil marriage between people of other faiths or no faith) is, of course, a good thing, but because Christ reveals something of the fullness of what it means to be human and to love, Christians believe that something more is possible in marriage between Christians (77). Similarly, in the loving relationships of Christians who are cohabiting, civilly married, or divorced and remarried, we can recognize the good elements that are no doubt present in all loving relationships, and yet call for deeper conversion (78–79). It is worth noting that the "back story" on the synod includes significant debate on the language used in this section. Some bishops worried about what people would think of "irregular" situations not being clearly condemned. Francis gives priority to mercy here, as he does in the document as a whole, while never failing to identify the ideal to which Catholics are called.

Finally, note the emphasis on children in paragraphs 80–85. Though marriage is "firstly an 'intimate partnership of life and love,'" married love "refuses every impulse to close in on itself; it is open to a fruitfulness that draws it beyond itself" (80). This language, a clear statement of theme five (love is fruitful) is a much more beautiful and expansive expression of the traditional teaching. It is designed to help people understand why Catholics care so much about children, but do not limit sacramental marriage to those who are able to conceive biologically. There are many ways to be fruitful.

This chapter succinctly lays out the basics of Catholic teaching, with an emphasis on spousal love. Attempts to use more appealing language rather than defend doctrine are sprinkled throughout the chapter. Still, Francis does even more to reach out to married couples in chapter 4.

Suggestions for Prayer

1. Meditate on how your marriage might be an icon for others. How could you improve?

2. Choose one of the less typical Scripture stories that Pope Francis uses to talk about family. Imagine yourself in the story. What do you see?

Discussion Questions

1. What is your experience of presentations of church teaching on procreation and contraception in sermons, classes,

retreats, and/or reading materials? Is Francis's presentation more effective?

2. After reading, how do you understand the difference between sacramental marriage and natural marriage? Does it make sense to you to say that the sacrament exists from the wedding day forward *and* that couples grow into the sacrament?

4 Looking In at Couples
Love in Marriage

Love does not have to be perfect for us to value it. The other person loves me as best they can, with all their limits, but the fact that love is imperfect does not mean that it is untrue or unreal. It is real, albeit limited and earthly.
—AL 113

This is the most "Pope Francis" chapter of AL, the heart of the document according to many commentators, the core of the "front story" he is most interested in communicating to married couples. It reads much more easily because the pope is drawing on sermons and experiential wisdom instead of quoting from synod documents and previous popes. He begins by setting himself a difficult task: saying something new about the familiar verses of 1 Corinthians 13:4-8 on the nature of love. But he succeeds because he is clearly thinking about people's real questions about marriage (the ones outlined in the beginning of chapter 3) and doing his best to answer them, not simply by going to Scripture but by pairing insights from many parts of the Christian tradition with insights clearly born of real-life experience.

A Virtue Ethic for Marriage

You might think of Pope Francis's meditation on 1 Corinthians 13 as a virtue ethic for marriage. Remember that the pope seeks to replace a negative, rule-based approach to the ethics of marriage and family with a positive ethic of ideals for which to strive. While it is nearly impossible to precisely define the nature of a virtue such as patience, describing what it is and what it is not is still helpful because it allows us to begin to perceive what the good life looks like. For Francis, patience is "more than a mere feeling" (AL 90–97). It is a stable quality of a person that allows him or her to practice restraint or not act on impulse. It is based on acceptance of the other as a person of equal worth and dignity. It requires a certain humility, a quality of not being "puffed up" or overimpressed with one's own importance. A patient person does not seek to dominate. The practice of not being rude, harsh, abrasive, or rigid is not simply a matter of good manners; it is rooted in respect. It entails being open to genuine encounter and peacemaking in the midst of difficult situations.

The meditation on the virtues related to love leads to a more extended discussion of the role of forgiveness in marriage. The pope is trying to argue that lasting love *is* possible and he is trying to describe the practices that make it possible. There is a strong challenge here to the commonly accepted wisdom that lasting love entails *finding* "the one." According to this story, if you find the right one, you were meant to be together, you fit together well, so your marriage just works. However, as one Christian theologian is fond of saying, everyone marries the wrong person.[1] To stay together, partners need to figure out how to *be* better together, and that entails learning how to forgive. This does not mean foregoing the "just desire to see our rights respected." Everyone deserves respect. But it does mean limiting judgment and giving up the "thirst for vengeance" (AL 105).

If this sort of radical forgiveness seems impossible, think of it as being rooted in God's forgiveness of human beings (108). Conscious that God sees the goodness of who we are despite our many imperfections, we can begin to see the failings of others as "part of a bigger picture" (113). People are complex combinations of strengths and weaknesses.

> To stay together, partners need to figure out how to *be* better together, and that entails learning how to forgive.

Note how Martin Luther King Jr.'s prophetic words about loving one's enemy are creatively marshaled here as words for married couples to live by.[2] Dr. King saw love of enemies as necessary for Christians for four reasons: God commands it, "returning hate for hate multiplies hate," "hate scars the soul and distorts the personality," and "love is the only force capable of transforming an enemy into a friend." Some would say this is a great ideal, but totally impractical. King believed this ideal was eminently practical. He gave three steps in answer to the question of how people can love their enemies:

1. Forgiveness must be initiated by the one who has been wronged. The wronged person does not ignore or sugarcoat the offense, but he does not allow the offense to get in the way of the relationship. He cancels the debt or lifts the burden in order to reconcile.

2. The forgiver recognizes that "the evil deed of the enemy-neighbor, the thing that hurts, never quite expresses all that he is . . . we know God's image is ineffably etched in his being."

3. Those who forgive never try to humiliate their enemies. The goal is reconciliation, not victory.

Couples, too, are called to see beyond each other's failings, and embrace hope, not despair (AL 116). They are called to embody "a love that never gives up" (119).

Every virtue ethic needs a vision of the good to orient it. Notice how Pope Francis echoes modern popes in his vision of marriage as intimate friendship (123). The language of what sociologists call "companionate marriage" is not prevalent in pre–Vatican II Catholic discourse on marriage, though it makes appearances here and there, even in figures such as Augustine and Aquinas. However, in the past it was much more common to hear marriage described as a contract, institution, or bond. Only in modern times do we have a sense of loving partnership as the heart of Christian marriage. Now, it makes sense to speak of "reciprocity, intimacy, warmth, stability and . . . a shared life," a commitment that is "all-encompassing," and of "mutual love" (125). Marriage is essentially a loving union, an icon that makes love visible (121), though in a fully human way, which means it is never perfect (122). The idea that loving couples can image or make real for others how much God loves human beings is pregnant with possibility and responsibility. In this vision, couples stay together for life not because of an external rule, but because of a "stable commitment to share and shape together the whole of life" (125).

Practices are another key to virtue ethics. Through intentional, regular actions, virtuous behavior becomes more and more a part of our character or who we really are. Note that the pope portrays sex as one of the practices that builds up virtues necessary to the loving friendship of marriage. There is a balance in this section of affirming the goodness of erotic passion and placing it in the context of a loving, lifelong relationship. It's important for the pope to underline the goodness of sexual passion, because so many Catholics still hear the church saying that sex is bad, unless it's for procreation. Still, if popular magazines offer advice about "how to keep the spark alive," encouraging married couples to re-create their dating days or learn new techniques, in the Catholic vision of sex, eros (desire) is good *and* always linked to agape (self-giving love). The both-and is important. It's not that desire is problematic so we have to be sure to moderate it with charity. It's that passionate desire fits in the framework of loving, lifelong relationships. If you want sex to be a practice that builds up marriage, it is important to know what your partner likes, but it is much more important to know and love your partner well.

Doesn't eroticism wane over time? The pope is realistic, but he is also making a claim in this section that passion and lifetime fidelity go together. The erotic passion that couples seek is an enduring passion that is always relational and "always directed to an ever more stable and intense union" (AL 125). Eros at its best invites two people deeper into relationship. It is good to desire to receive pleasure as well as give pleasure (157), to luxuriate in ecstasy as the mystics saw themselves resting in God's passionate embrace (125). But good couples also develop a "mature spontaneity" (151), which may at times mean adjusting one's own wants and needs in light of a partner's desires (152). The practice of sex envisioned here is marked by the virtues described earlier in this section: patience, humility, and love.

The pope's focus on the practices of marriage, or the cultivation of love, is not limited to sex. Instead of just saying, "Stay married!" he narrates the day-to-day process of being in a loving relationship. He encourages appreciating and even contemplating one's beloved (127), taking joy in bringing the other delight (129). In what may be the first movie reference in a papal document, he gives the example of the famous scene in the movie *Babette's Feast*, which shows the preparation of an elaborate meal for beloved friends.

Because this section clearly draws on the experiences of married couples, it is a virtue ethic marked by realism. There is a recognition that the joy of love can continue even through pain and sorrow (130). Choosing the word "joy" over "pleasure" or "happiness," the pope insists, "Marital joy can be experienced even amid sorrow; it involves accepting that marriage is an inevitable mixture of enjoyment and struggles, tensions and repose, pain and relief, satisfactions and longings, annoyances and pleasures" (126). Mature couples know that their marriage need not collapse during difficult times, but can endure and thrive. They know the importance of cultivating love through all of the ups and downs of life, with loving words and actions (133). They know that marriage must grow or die, and they know that growth entails risk (134–35). And risk might bring new life. Yet, mature couples also know better than to expect too much. Being realistic is important.

> Mature couples know that their marriage need not collapse during difficult times, but can endure and thrive.

Couples also know that maintaining relationships requires attending to the practice of communication (136–41). Notice the detailed discussion about what it means to listen well to another person, spending enough time, showing affection, acknowledging the other's truth and legitimacy of his or her concerns and insights, having an open mind, being willing to change, and, interestingly enough, cultivating oneself so that one has something interesting to say, something valuable to bring to the dialogue! This very specific narration of communication paints a down-to-earth picture of a vibrant and loving relationship.

Internal Problems

The pope is not unaware of the very real problems even the happiest married couples ordinarily face but he insists that *even when* marriage is not thrilling; when a partner is annoying, unattractive, or sick; when it seems that maybe you married the wrong person, "Love opens our eyes and enables us to see, beyond all else, the great worth of a human being" (AL 128). These are the ordinary challenges of long-term relationships and there are plenty of long-married couples that can attest to the possibility of overcoming these challenges and finding greater fulfillment over time.

But not all problems are normal and to be expected. Some relationships are distorted in more profound ways and violence "contradicts the very nature of the conjugal union" (AL 154).[3] Notice that the pope is particularly concerned about the misuse of power or domination (156). He calls for trust, not control (115); for appreciation, not possession (127). Though other popes have briefly touched upon domestic violence in documents on women or family, Pope Francis addresses the topic in a more sustained and substantial way. He is clearly aware of how pervasive it is. Globally, 30 percent of women have experienced family violence and 38 percent of all murders of women are committed by their partners. Rates of violence are highest in the developing world and lower overall in high-income areas, but no area of the world is immune.[4] Family life across the globe is marred by violence, both physical and sexual. Francis contrasts sexual manipulation with truly human sex, which is always mutual (AL 154).

Significantly, he anticipates objections to men's right to "rule" the household (still widespread throughout the world), arguing that calls for wifely submission cannot be supported by Ephesians 5:22 ("Wives should be subordinate to their husbands . . ."). Rather, he, like John Paul II before him, reinterprets this passage and defines *reciprocal* self-gift as the heart of marriage. Unlike John Paul II, he does not differentiate the roles of men and women with respect to this passage. Instead, he redefines self-gift as the practice of being "constantly mindful of others," and insists this practice is to be embraced by men and women (156). At this point in the document (157), he identifies violence as a profound distortion, but only later will he address the subjects of separation, divorce, and remarriage.

Why Forever?

Here the pope is setting out the ideal, a vision of indissolubility to inspire and orient couples that marry in the church. In sum, it is this: committing to lifelong marriage is the only way to attain the depth of loving relationships we are made for. This is human experience: depth comes over the long haul, not in momentary intense connections. In spite of all we know about the difficulties of sustaining marriage, people seek lifelong marriages for themselves, parents hope that their children will have lifelong marriages, and children hope their parents will stay together for life. This is because, Catholics believe, "it is in the very nature of conjugal love to be definitive" (AL 123). This, not "to stay together *unless* . . . ," is what we promise in our vows (124).

Marriage is not just a piece of paper. The promise to love another person forever "protects and shapes a shared commitment to deeper growth," gives to love a visible form, and publicly identifies one person with another. Though appropriately rooted in emotion, a marriage vow comes with obligations (131). It is a risky promise for two people to make, but the vow "protects the 'yes'" they give each other, because with this promise, they can trust that "they will never be abandoned" (132). With this promise of "mutual belonging," two individuals become partners, forever companions on life's journey (163). This is the very heart of the "front story" of The Joy of Love.

Suggestions for Prayer

1. Meditate on the idea of "cultivating love." Where in your marriage is growth needed? What would it take for growth to happen?

2. When have you felt the love or forgiveness of your spouse beyond what you deserve? Recall the depth of that experience and spend some time in gratitude.

Discussion Questions

1. Does it make sense to you to see lifelong fidelity as a necessary framework for deep love?

2. Can the pope's strong words on forgiveness be squared with his warnings about the distortions of domination and violence?

5 Looking Outward with Couples
Love Made Fruitful

We also do well to remember that procreation and adoption are not the only ways of experiencing the fruitfulness of love. Even large families are called to make their mark on society, finding other expressions of fruitfulness that in some way prolong the love that sustains them. . . . Families should not see themselves as a refuge from society, but instead go forth from their homes in a spirit of solidarity with others. In this way, they become a hub for integrating persons . . .
—AL 181

In chapter 4, we saw Pope Francis looking at marriage with the internal experiences of couples in mind. He provided a thick description of how married love looks and feels from the inside and an argument for sustaining it over a lifetime (theme one: the goodness of intimacy). But in chapter 5, the pope asks readers to look beyond intimacy. Marriage in the Catholic tradition is about more than two people, however much in love those two may be. But if marriage for Catholics isn't just about procreation (right?), what is this "more" that Catholic marriage is about? In this chapter, Pope Francis explains theme five: love is fruitful.

The section begins with a simple claim, "Love always gives life" (AL 165). It may not seem like a radical claim, but when juxtaposed with popular cultural narratives, it is distinct. In the movies, couples marry because they are in love and the happily ever after is all about their joy. If that joy includes kids, great, but if they're happy with dogs and careers, that's fine, too. Couples in the Catholic tradition are called to love each other well, but, as John Paul II said, love "does not end with the couple" (quoted in AL 165). Love overflows. Notice how Francis moves from a more traditional discussion of fruitfulness reflected in birth and parenting to less typical discussions of extended family, the role of families as servants in the world, and the scandal of inequality to which socially conscious Christian families need to be attentive.

Parenting

Even the more traditional discussion of fruitfulness by parenting is marked by the inclusion of creation, adoption, and baptism. Pope Francis wants to affirm the widely shared desire to have children while also outlining a distinctive Christian vision of children. A child, he insists, is always a gift to be welcomed, never a mistake to be regretted (AL 166). From the earliest days of life, each child "has a place in God's heart," and parents share in the joy and mystery of creation (168, 171). Adoption is not a lesser path but a way for married couples to be fruitful, "a very generous way to become parents" (179). Of course, birth parents, too, are generous in sharing the children they cannot care for alone. Both birth parents and adoptive parents can be channels of God's love. From a Christian perspective, biological connection is important, but the most important thing is for children to be accepted and loved (180).

All parents have dreams for their children, but Christians entrust their children to God in baptism (169). Children are not our possessions; ultimately they belong to God. Parents are called to "accept their child fully and wholeheartedly," love children unconditionally, not because of anything children embody or do, but just because they are children (170). There is no mandate here to have as many children as possible.

> All parents have dreams for their children, but Christians entrust their children to God in baptism.

"Large families are a joy for the Church," but Pope Francis is less adamant than previous popes about encouraging large families. Instead, he remarks that even these generous families are not excused from a more expansive obligation of fruitfulness (167).

To become a parent entails much more than conceiving a child. The pope addresses both mothers and fathers in his discussion of the kind of love children need and deserve (172–77). He will have more to say in chapter 7 on child rearing, but in this chapter he focuses on the parents' role in assuring that children see and experience love.

His words on the specific functions and roles of mothers and fathers are distinctive in the contemporary Catholic tradition. While John Paul II and Benedict XVI are perceived as more traditional in their thinking, neither devoted as much time as Francis does here to distinguishing the roles of male and female parents and insisting that children deserve both a mother and a father.

Here, some "back story" is important. During the synods, some conservative Catholics worried that insufficient attention was being given to the defense of traditional marriage between a man and a woman. A group of Catholic scholars wrote an open letter to Pope Francis, urging him to focus on providing a strong argument for indissoluble heterosexual marriage open to procreation.[1] Conservative Catholics were often critical of the reports coming out of the synods, especially the midterm report in 2014, which was substantially revised following its controversial reception. Traditional groups highlighted their concerns at the 2015 World Meeting of Families in Philadelphia and the Humanum Conference held directly after the 2015 synod in Rome. A flurry of books and articles defending traditional marriage were released to respond to progressive attempts to argue for greater welcome and acceptance of those who do not fully live up to Catholic ideals.

Pope Francis's response to the concerns of these groups consists of these seven paragraphs, as well as several other paragraphs scattered throughout the document in which the value of complementarity is underlined. His perspective allows for the acceptance of feminism, as long as it does not "negate motherhood" (AL 173) (as no feminist I know of does!), and for "a certain flexibility of roles and responsibilities," as long as the necessity of both male and female is accepted (175). His affirmation of traditional roles seems to be an argument for traditional marriage.

As you read, you might think about whether or not his descriptions accurately reflect the diversity of marriages you know as well as whether couples that do not fit the model (e.g., a more nurturing father who is the primary caregiver for his children or a more competitive mother who is the primary breadwinner for her family) would necessarily be less effective as parents. It would also be helpful to compare this section with the assertion in chapter 7 that because masculinity and femininity are "not rigid categories," there is no need to overemphasize gender difference or adopt rigid roles, which might in fact hinder the freedom and harm the development of children, especially those who don't fit into a particular mold (286).

Francis's defense of traditional marriage is followed by two sections that expand the definition and scope of family.

Servants in the World

The first expands the scope of what Catholics call fruitfulness. Parenting is but one way a couple's love spills over into the world. The pope challenges the idea that the family should be a refuge from the world. We can imagine his response to the contemporary real estate ads, so many of which emphasize a huge master bedroom, bath, and sitting room as a place of retreat from the world's cares, with spa-like amenities and luxurious finishes that are "a dream come true."

> The pope challenges the idea that the family should be a refuge from the world.

Pope Francis asks couples to "go forth from their homes in a spirit of solidarity with others" (AL 181). This message is consistent in contemporary Catholic social thought. Spend some time thinking about the Mario Benedetti poem the pope quotes to capture the idea of love animated by concern for others. The poet captures a Christian love that appreciates the beauty of a spouse's commitment to work for justice. He paints a picture of a companionship of two who work together for something larger than themselves, who can say, "We are much more than just two" (quoted in AL 181). And this idealistic paragraph is followed by a cautionary paragraph urging families not to see themselves as perfect, not to be remote from others or make others "feel looked down upon or judged" (182). So it is clear that the social mission of the family should be perceived as a call to servanthood. Just like any other dimension of family life, no family will realize the vision perfectly.

And yet, the urgency of the social task is real. Listen to Pope Francis talk about spouses "who experience the power of love" and "know that this love is called to bind the wounds of the outcast, to foster a culture of encounter and to fight for justice" (AL 183). Families, no less than single people, are called to live out the most radical passages of the gospel: the Sermon on the Mount (Matt 5–7), the parable of the Last Judgment (Matt 25:31-46), and the parable in which Jesus calls for inviting the poor and the outcast to a feast (Luke 14:12-14). "Here is the secret to a happy family," the pope says.

Scandal

The evangelizing role of the family is through witness, which is not primarily the shape of the family but by how they live (AL 184). Francis is clear: families may give scandal by their way of life. Paul's famous passage about the community in Corinth where the rich enjoyed luxury while the poor went hungry is creatively applied to families. Pope Francis, the pope of mercy who has made such an impression with his own simple lifestyle and commitment to spending time with the poor, makes it clear that these are the kinds of questions he wants families to wrestle with. "How fruitful are we, really?" we all might ask.

Extended Family

This section concludes with lengthy reflections on the extended family (AL 187–98). The concern to provide a family ethic encompassing the relationships of a variety of family members can be seen as a further broadening of the definition of family. The pope knows that all of us are family members, even if we are not married. The obligations of being a son or daughter, brother or sister, in-law, aunt or uncle, grandparent, grandchild, and friend are also important. To have "family values" must mean reaching out in appropriate ways to family members, especially those with greater needs, those who are alone, and "even those who have made shipwreck of their lives" (197). There is strong encouragement here to develop and strengthen the bonds not just of husbands and wives but of families as networks of kin with a special responsibility to the weaker among them, so that they attain "ever deeper and more intense communion" (196).

This section is all about looking out. It is pushing couples to think beyond the romance of intimacy to a passion for giving: in the birthing or adopting and raising of children, in nurturing relationships throughout the extended family, and in embracing the social mission of the family. The focus on fruitfulness in chapter 5 complements the focus on intimacy in chapter 4. Together, these sections set out the Catholic vision of marriage for a skeptical audience: Christian marriage involves a lifelong covenant that allows for trust, depth, and belonging. That same love provides a strong foundation for an outward gaze. Marriage, love, and justice go together.

Suggestions for Prayer

1. Meditate on the passages Francis highlights in paragraph 183. What would it mean for your family to respond to the challenges of those stories?

2. What aspects of parenting do you do well? Where might growth be needed? What kind of parent do you really want to be? To what extent have you been able to be this parent?

Discussion Questions

1. The social mission of the family is challenging. Is it fair to ask families to take up this task, given other responsibilities and pressures? Is it possible, given the diversity within

families, for families to make serving the poor and outcast central to their lives?

2. What sort of "scandal" is typical of families in your community? Are there families living differently who suggest a different model is possible?

APPLYING

How Can We Accompany Those in Imperfect Situations?

If in part 2 Pope Francis speaks directly to married couples and draws upon their life wisdom, part 3 is more directed to ministers and their challenges. When priests and other church insiders commented on AL, they focused on chapters 6 and 8. Those deeply invested in the controversy over the possibility of communion for divorced and remarried Catholics wanted to know if Francis settled the issue. Parish priests who minister to many in "irregular" marriages or living situations wanted to know if anything had changed. Everyone was talking about a new "tone," initiated by Pope Francis, but what would that mean, practically speaking, for everyday parish life?

The pope frequently uses the metaphor of "field hospital" to talk about how the church must go to those who are most in need. How might that model of church shape the way local parishes approach marriage? Chapter 6 tries to answer these questions. Chapter 7, which focuses on raising children, offers a compelling, somewhat countercultural vision of Christian parenting that could be supported by parishes if they redirected their energy. Chapter 8 focuses on pastoral care of the divorced and remarried, with brief comments on other groups in need of attention and welcome. In each of these chapters, despite tackling some more technical issues, Pope Francis tries to bring his trademark mercy and joy, driving home theme three: *Christians accompany those who experience brokenness or failure in marriage.*

6 Can the Church Be a Field Hospital for Families?

The dialogue that took place during the Synod raised the need for new pastoral methods. I will attempt to mention some of these in a very general way. Different communities will have to devise more practical and effective initiatives that respect both the Church's teaching and local problems and needs. Without claiming to present a pastoral plan for the family, I would now like to reflect on some more significant pastoral challenges.
—AL 199

Accompaniment is not a common word in church documents. However, it is a word Pope Francis has been using since the beginning of his pontificate. Accompaniment is the work of the field hospital.[1] It means to walk with or be with. It is often associated with Latin American theology, participatory models of economic development, and service or immersion trips. It captures the idea that when we go to people in need, we do not pretend to have all the answers to their problems and we don't tell them what to do with their lives. We are not there to save them. We and they have gifts to offer and things that need fixing. We begin by listening and walking beside people, appreciating their wisdom and learning their story. We ask what they need and what we might be able to help them accomplish. We hope that our encounter will lead to needed change in our lives as well.

Pope Francis has brought accompaniment into Catholic moral theology for the first time. In *Evangelii Gaudium*, he introduced it.[2] It became a central concern of the synods, shifting the conversation from doctrine to action. In AL, Francis officially brings accompaniment to family ethics. But notice the opening quote in this section. Though the pope aims to discuss pastoral challenges and provide some guidance, he is committed to leaving as much decision-making power as possible in the hands of local communities. This commitment is rooted in a concern for "pushing the power down" after decades of concentrated efforts to push more and more power into the hands of the Vatican. He offers direction, not one-size-fits-all rules.

The original focus of the synod on the family was the role of the family in the task of evangelization. As it turned out, there was much more discussion at the synod on challenges families face and how the church could better accompany families. In the beginning of chapter 6, the pope is trying to show how important the latter is to the former. If priests and lay ministers do not understand what families are facing, they won't be able to help them deal with major challenges or "take up their role as active agents" in the world (AL 200). The pope is aware that the pre-synod surveys revealed a need for better training of priests and ministers (202–4), who need to learn not just doctrine or canon law but the reality of family life. If the church wants families to be and do more, it has to learn how to accompany families.

If the church wants families to be and do more, it has to learn how to accompany families.

With an accompaniment model, the church may be better able to embody the field hospital Pope Francis so often talks about, by going to those who are most broken, providing mercy and healing, and being open to a deeper understanding of what marriage and family are all about.

Marriage Preparation

One key to helping people face the challenges of family life is better marriage preparation. In reading the pope's thoughts on what good preparation should look like (AL 205–11), you might think, "When people are preparing to marry, what are they doing? What can the church do to help them with this task?" Because if for Christians, finding "the one" is not most important, if for us, *being* "the one" is more crucial, we have to be serious about forming people who can in fact *be* "the one" for the people they love. The pope's inclusion of the virtues in his discussion of marriage preparation implies the need for character formation along with religious formation (206). Couples "do not need to be taught the entire Catechism," but they do need to be presented with an attractive vision of marriage worth striving for (207). The specific formation preceding marriage is meant to build on a lifetime of character formation that comes from witnessing the lives of married couples (208).

Notice the focus on helping couples know their partners well, be realistic, and discern their own readiness for the sacrifice marriage entails (209–12). This preparation, rooted in pastoral knowledge of marital breakups, presents a counter-narrative to cultural engagement rituals, which often focus on storybook-like proposals, idealized engagement photos, and elaborate wedding plans. Parishes need to figure out how to use this important time to prepare couples to "embark upon marriage as a lifelong calling based on a firm and realistic decision to face all trials and difficult moments together" (211).

When it comes to preparing the marriage liturgy, the pope exhorts couples, "Have the courage to be different," by focusing on "the love you share," and "opting for a more modest and simple celebration" (212). He wants them to contemplate the words of consent and the bodily consummation that, according to the Catholic tradition, will bind them together forever (213). He tasks parish ministers with shepherding couples through a better formation process.

The pope has worried some by saying that many couples do not really understand what they are doing when they get married, that they do not "grasp the theological and spiritual import of the words of consent, which . . . involve a totality that includes the future: 'until death do us part'" (AL 214).[3] Francis tries to remedy this problem by explaining the idea that a promise of one's whole self can only be a forever promise. Note that he asks couples to consider praying or meditating on biblical passages together, and encourages priests to think of wedding ceremonies (which many are not so excited about) as opportunities to share the Catholic vision of marriage and the joy of the gospel (AL 216). He calls attention to the problem of limited understanding and offers suggestions for helping couples fully grasp what the church asks of them. Still, he knows that accompaniment does not end with the wedding.

> A promise of one's whole self can only be a forever promise.

Accompaniment in the Early Years

The pope devotes significant time to the challenges couples face in the early years of marriage, with the hope of helping ministers envision how they can better accompany young families (AL 217–30). The vision of marriage he presents is realistic and dynamic. Marriage, the pope says, "is not something that happens once for all." When they marry, couples "assume an active and creative role in a lifelong project" (218). They build their marriage up day by day. Each spouse is a "work in progress" and together they are charged with overcoming all obstacles that stand in the way of their goal. With hope, they "keep dancing towards the future" (219). As their love grows, matures, and deepens, they learn how to give way, negotiate, and compromise (220). Throughout this section, the pope returns to common themes he thinks need to be better communicated: realism, marriage as a process, the need for change on the part of both spouses, and their role in "forming" each other.

Pope Francis's thoughts here echo the theology of Richard Gaillardetz, who calls marriage "a crucible" of salvation. Like the pope, Gaillardetz tries to temper unrealistic expectations. He wants couples to embrace the daring adventure of committing to a costly relationship that will require them to empty themselves for the other person. The need for sacrifice is not a mark of a bad relationship but a sign of two different people who have to work very hard to grow into deeper unity and, in the process, become better people before God. Gaillardetz claims that his wife is his "salvation."[4] It is important to qualify this claim by noting that submitting to a partner's dominating, belittling, or violent actions is not a healthy kind of sacrifice. Still, for most couples, acceptance of sacrifice for the sake of the marriage and each person is crucial.

In the paragraphs that follow, everyday problems of spouses are described (e.g., decisions about how many children to welcome, integrating religious practices into a home [especially if one spouse is not a believer], the difficulty of finding time for each other, etc.). Ideas for parish programs are offered (e.g., talks, workshops, counseling, mentor couples, associations), but because the pope is following the open method we discussed at the outset of this chapter, he does not proscribe, but only suggests, leaving it to each community to figure out how best to walk with married couples.

Importantly, when he discusses family planning (AL 222), he encourages generosity in relation to new life and quotes the Catechism's promotion of natural methods. But he prefaces this reference to church teaching with a long discussion, buttressed by selective quotation from *Humanae Vitae*, on good, conscience-based decision making in this area. The negative judgments about couples that use artificial contraception, so frequent in the previous two pontificates, do not appear. Instead, a more positive emphasis on the gift of children is adopted and couples are trusted to make the decisions that are right for them. If some parishes have been overly preoccupied with artificial contraception, Pope Francis calls for a shift in attention to the everyday challenges couples face.

Separation and Divorce

When are challenges significant enough to warrant separation or divorce? The pope questions the popular notion that a lack of satisfaction or fulfillment constitutes a reason to part, in order to help ministers do the same. This notion can be easily dismissed, as most would say divorce is only justified in serious cases, but a closer look at popular film and literature reveals a disturbing prevalence of narratives constructed around a lack of fulfillment storyline. The text offers another lens through which to view difficulties. A crisis, the pope suggests, can be seen as an opportunity to speak "heart to heart," "an apprenticeship in growing closer together or learning a little more about what it means to be married" (AL 232). Aware that most troubled couples do not seek pastoral help from their parishes, he asks ministers to find a new approach that will encourage them to do so. His strategy is to build up confidence in the church as a resource by showing awareness of difficulties, while maintaining that love can be revived and renewed (237).

Though wanting to encourage couples to stay together, the pope knows that this will not be possible in situations of "grave injustice, violence or chronic ill-treatment" (241), so he also encourages better accompaniment of those who divorce. Some needed reforms in annulment procedures have already been initiated and the pope encourages dioceses to quickly implement the new guidelines (244). With continuing respect for varied contexts, he encourages the development of ministries for troubled couples and their children. But his key concerns are how spouses and children are treated. On spouses, his strongly worded comments prior to the beginning of the 2015 synod of bishops are repeated twice here: the divorced, even those who remarry, should not feel as though they have been excommunicated (AL 243, 246).[5] According to canon law, they are *not* automatically excommunicated, but, especially when they are unable to participate in the Eucharist, they often feel as if they are. The pope all but demands changes in pastoral practice to address this problem.

However, he does not forget the children of divorced spouses who "often suffer in silence" (AL 246). Because children are the most vulnerable people involved in a divorce, he asks that their needs be prioritized. Helping couples embrace the challenge of child-centered decision making in the midst of family breakdown then becomes an additional responsibility of pastoral ministers.

During the synod, when the suffering of divorced adults became a central focus of the bishops' dialogue, critics worried that the suffering of children was being ignored. Some adult children of divorce even wrote an article in *America* magazine, arguing for maintaining the exclusion of divorced and remarried people from the Eucharist in order to recognize the ongoing sin of a second union and the pain it causes, especially in the lives of the children of divorced parents.[6] The pope (as we will see in chapter

8) seems to desire a change in eucharistic practice, but he does not forget the children's pain. He asks parishes to accompany both adults and children in broken families.

Interreligious Marriage

Though divorce is the central issue of this section (as it was at the synods), other related family problems that warrant the church responding as a field hospital are briefly addressed. Interreligious or interfaith couples in diverse contexts are understood to have special needs, as are married couples in which one person is not Catholic (AL 248–49). These situations exist not only in the United States and Europe, and other developed countries where religious pluralism is high and unbelief is on the rise, but also in developing countries where traditional religions, evangelical churches, and Islam claim significant portions of the population. Addressing this reality is important to authentic pastoral practice. It is not helpful to assume that everyone is Catholic. Similarly, single-parent families (252) and families in which a spouse has died (253–58) are highlighted as cases deserving special care. Throughout, Francis keeps the focus off theological argument and on walking with couples in need.

Same-Sex Unions

Same-sex relationships were the subject of some controversy at the 2014 synod. The initial midterm report from that meeting stirred up vigorous debate with its claim that such relationships, like marriages, could embody virtues of love and self-sacrifice. It was later modified, and the final report was modified yet again, though it still signaled some attempt to move beyond the current rhetoric. Many Catholic laypeople and some bishops want the church to move in this direction but many more, especially in the global South, do not. Same-sex relationships fell off the main agenda in the 2015 synod and the language of the midterm report does not appear in AL.

Characteristically, the pope begins the brief section (250–51) with the merciful love of Jesus that the church is called to make its own. He repeats official teaching on the dignity of each person and the duty of nondiscrimination. However, he also uses the phrase "persons who experience same-sex attraction" instead of "gay or lesbian persons" (which is more typical in his ordinary speech and less hurtful to those in the GLBTQ community). He quotes a particularly controversial passage from a 2003 document of the Vatican's Congregation for the Doctrine of the Faith, which suggests a total lack of similarity between same-sex union and marriage, an assertion that many Catholics who know same-sex couples find puzzling, at the very least.

Though some Catholics hoped that more openness to same-sex unions would emerge from the synod and from the pope who famously said of homosexual persons, "Who am I to judge?" it appears that there was not enough momentum for the bishops to move in that direction.[7] Though the subject is only directly addressed in these two paragraphs, Pope Francis does not move the church forward on this issue as he does on other issues. What he does do, in keeping with his consistent desire to keep peace among the bishops and keep our focus on mercy, is characterize gay and lesbian people, along with all those who struggle to accept and live out church teaching, as people who need the church to be a field hospital. He asks parishes to figure out how to better welcome and accompany them along with everyone else who has experienced the church less often as a place of healing and more often as a place of judgment.

In sum, chapter 6 is all about the church reaching out and becoming a field hospital for families. There are some passages that continue the "front story" line of helping married couples sustain lifelong marriages, but much of the chapter is written for ministers, to encourage better accompaniment at the parish level. Make no mistake—Pope Francis is calling them to change the way they do business, so that parishes better embody the love of Christ and the joy of the Gospel.

Suggestions for Prayer

1. If you have experienced or are experiencing problems in your family, reflect on those problems in the context of the idea of crisis as apprenticeship or an opportunity to grow.

2. If you are married, reflect back to your own marriage preparation process and early years of marriage. What challenges did you face? What or who helped you along the way? How might you be called to accompany others today?

Discussion Questions

1. Think of a movie that tells the story of a marriage breaking apart (and perhaps a new relationship beginning). How would the couple's story be challenged by the pope's claims in this section? How might his claims be challenged?

2. Have you experienced the church as a field hospital? Have you experienced a lack of welcome and healing? Is welcome and accompaniment enough or is change in the church's understanding of some of the situations discussed in this chapter necessary?

7 Can the Church Help Parents Raise Their Children Well?

[I]t is more important to start processes than to dominate spaces.
—AL 261

Freedom is the primary concern of chapter 7, which makes sense, because if you come across a group of parents talking about children, chances are, they'll be talking about freedom. Should an infant be fed on a schedule or allowed to nurse as much as he wants? Is a toddler better off with a scheduled day at preschool or should she have freedom to do as she pleases at home? Is it better to raise "free-range" kids who can make their way around the block and eventually the city or do kids need more adult supervision? Is the freedom (over schedules) and control (over curriculum) of homeschooling good for kids and families? What about curfews, dating, extracurriculars, friends, money, Sunday Mass, or choosing a college major? The tough parenting questions all center on freedom.

The pope asks parents to think about how they are helping kids "grow in freedom, maturity, overall discipline and real autonomy" (AL 261). In the background seems to be a worry that some parents (and perhaps some Christian parenting resources) emphasize control, obedience, and "dominating spaces." There is ample data showing that authoritarian parenting like this does not yield particularly good outcomes. More importantly, the pope suggests it is not in keeping with Christian understandings of the role of freedom in moral life. Instead of dominating, Pope Francis recommends trying to really understand, be affectionate toward, respect, and influence children. His approach to parenting is consistent with his general approach to the moral life.

In chapter 4, married couples were given an approach to marriage rooted in the virtues and in chapter 7, the pope offers a virtue ethics approach to parenting. Families should be defined not by rules, but by virtues. Of course, some rules are necessary for running a household and respecting the limitations of children, but the pope's point here is that true moral formation doesn't happen through obedience to rules. He encourages parents to think more deeply about how they can use dialogue and activity to encourage good habits and build good character in their children. Stifling freedom doesn't work, but channeling freedom is still important. He offers this brief primer as a way of accompanying parents in their most important and challenging task.

> Families should be defined not by rules, but by virtues.

A Virtue Ethic for Parents

The key claim of this section is that parents will do better by providing opportunities for their children to grow in virtue than imposing virtue from the top down. "The virtuous life thus builds, strengthens and shapes freedom, lest we become slaves of dehumanizing and antisocial inclinations" (AL 267). For example, the practice of gathering for a family meal encourages discipline, community, and respect for others. Children can learn to wait until others come to the table to eat, and to tolerate meals that may not be their favorites because they know others' tastes differ from theirs. If a family maintains a practice of turning off phones and TV, they learn to be mindful about technology, though they might make an exception to include a family member who is out of town, utilizing technology to sustain family ties (278). In conversation at the table, family members can learn to ask about someone else's day, listen to a story, extend a line of conversation, and engage political and cultural ideas. Eating together can help children interiorize virtues and bind a family closer together. All of this can help children and adults become more able to resist the "dehumanizing and antisocial inclinations" of an overly individualistic society.

Families can intentionally cultivate virtue through the practice of family meals in several ways. Instead of preaching or imposing, they can adopt practices that embody their values. For instance, they can choose low-cost foods to avoid luxury and make room for charity, eat less meat and dairy (and prioritize humanely raised meat and dairy) out of respect for animals, and eat mostly whole foods that require little processing (such as legumes and produce) in order to minimize their impact on the earth. These are simple ways to connect family life with ecological virtues. On these and other issues, the idea is to avoid negativity, and instead hold up exemplars who motivate and values worth striving for (272).

Of course, children won't necessarily adopt all of the values their parents introduce. Spouses, too, may disagree, and may remain unconvinced by a partner's attempts to apprentice them into a new way of thinking! The pope encourages a "patient realism" that does not demand too much and the acceptance of "small steps" toward the ideals parents want their children to adopt.

Here some "back story" may be helpful. Although the pope does not use the word, "gradualism" seems relevant to the approach to his virtue ethic of parenting. The idea that some will proceed gradually or slowly toward moral ideals was controversial at the 2014 synod.[1] The term appeared in the 2014 midterm report but, after much discussion, it received far less attention in the final report. Some bishops asserted that people might only gradually come to accept and live up to the church's teaching on cohabitation, contraception, remarriage, or same-sex marriage, but could be encouraged in their partial attempts to live out moral ideals in the meantime. Some bishops thought of this as practical wisdom, while others worried about a watering down of moral norms.

The idea of gradualism appears in chapter 7 as a crucial part of doing moral formation without alienation. Francis is simply asserting that children, like most people, don't respond well to ultimatums or impossible ideals. But when they feel respected, they become more willing to take small steps toward ideals that may be very difficult to maintain. Gradually, they may be able to do more and more. Parents who accept moral formation as a gradual process can help their children channel their freedom in good directions (AL 273). Values accepted in freedom are then more likely to be maintained over time. By embracing a virtue ethic with room for growth, Francis intends to provide support for families whose efforts to practice virtue may be partial in the beginning but stronger over time.

Beyond Self-Absorption to Solidarity

Still, if Francis supports respecting children's freedom, he is not suggesting allowing children to do whatever they want. Part of parenting is helping children learn to be critical of mainstream culture and he aims to encourage parents in their efforts along these lines (AL 274). The pope uses the beautiful image popularized at Vatican II of the family as "a school for human enrichment" (*Gaudium et Spes* 52). He advocates helping children cultivate attraction for some values and repugnance for others. For example, to return to the family meal, popular advertisements might glamorize hamburgers without acknowledging the animal suffering or environmental degradation involved in beef production. Shedding light on this practice and helping children cultivate a taste for healthy vegetarian or less-meat meals can be a part of countercultural Christian parenting.

One of the most important family values Francis emphasizes is moving beyond "self-absorption" (AL 276). Interestingly, this value is important both in social ethics and sexual ethics. The pope starts discussing it with reference to social ethics. In families we learn to wait, to not give in to every impulse. This happens naturally, "through the demands made by life in common" (275). When we share space, cars, food, and stuff with others, we cannot have everything we want all the time. Freed from too much focus on the self, we can move to concern for others (276). From here, we can begin to rethink habits of consumption, our impact on the environment, and our response to human suffering (277). Again, the table can be helpful, for example, if families take the opportunity to pray not only for their own concerns but for the concerns of neighbors and strangers, and if they spend some time in discussion of global events, especially those affecting the most vulnerable human beings.

The move beyond self-absorption is also relevant to the cultivation of a good, healthy sexual ethic. Because sex is so often "trivialized and impoverished," it is important for families to provide an alternative vision (280). The virtue language provided in this section is an alternative to the reductionism of the right (Just say no) and left (Have safe sex). The worries expressed here are not so much about the breaking of rules but about the significant moral issues that often accompany the rule breaking. Francis provides a framework for talking to children and adolescents about sex in a new way suited to a new age. He asks parents to lead with what they want for their kids: self-knowledge, self-control, and the development of "capacities for joy and loving encounter" (280). He wants parents to help children avoid "the things that cripple their capacity for love" (281). Modesty of dress and gaze is important because using or objectifying people is wrong (282), though that doesn't mean adolescents can't strive to dress attractively and appreciate physical beauty.

Note that the emphasis throughout this section is on teaching children not just how to "say no" but how to love well. This entails cultivating sensitivity, care, respect, and communication skills (283). To give oneself to another with one's body is a very big deal. The pope borrows from psychologist Erich Fromm the term "patient apprenticeship," and asks parents to help their children prepare to give themselves authentically. This will mean taking young people seriously, not dismissing their loves or their desires, and preparing them "for a great and generous love" (284). Without dismissing the difficulty of this task, Francis is trying to provide assistance to parents so that they can help their children become sexually virtuous, which includes being good and generous lovers who are other-focused rather than self-absorbed.

Passing on the Faith

The final section of chapter 7 is similar in its high expectations and its refusal to fall into platitudes. Christian documents for families often approach the subject of passing on the faith with an unhelpful naïveté. There is a sense that if parents would simply mandate the correct ritual practices (e.g., Mass attendance, along with the rosary, eucharistic adoration, and/or Scripture reading), children will be inspired practitioners of Catholicism for life. Some early Christian thinkers even insisted that parents were responsible for their children's acceptance of the faith and would be damned if they failed in passing on the faith, but those days are long gone! The pre-synod surveys revealed a strong concern of parents (and grandparents) about the difficulty of this task in the current cultural context. The pope writes with those struggles in mind, offering accompaniment without judgment.

Note that the task is described as "faith formation" rather than "keeping kids Catholic" or ensuring that they go to Mass. The pope addresses both mothers and fathers, and suggests a wide variety of options, including cultural rituals and practices, formal prayer, and parish involvement. The distinctive challenge of faith formation for adolescents is understood, and here again we find Pope Francis's insistent emphasis on sharing the beauty and passion of the faith rather than imposing rules.

Near the end of the discussion, he returns to the theme of the family's role in evangelization, but note his emphasis. He asserts that a family animated by faith will want to share it with others, perhaps formally, but more typically by the witness of their lives. He quotes from the 2015 synod report, which beautifully recounts the ways a family testifies to Christian faith, in "solidarity with the poor, openness to a diversity of people, the protection of creation," and so forth (290). If the family has "schooled" itself in deeper humanity, its practices can make it a kind of sacrament in the world, an icon of the power of love. This is a tall order, but in providing this vision, the pope resituates parenting in the larger context of gospel values and the central Christian task of discipleship (theme five: love is fruitful). It is in the practices and processes of family life centered on love of others, and not in simple obedience to rules, that families become Christian.

Though the vision is demanding, the pope hopes that his encouragement will be taken up by parishes as

> If the family has "schooled" itself in deeper humanity, its practices can make it a kind of sacrament in the world, an icon of the power of love.

they begin to figure out how to help married men and women with their most daunting task. In community, with the respect and support of ministers and other adults who struggle with the same things they do, parents may feel better equipped to raise children well.

Suggestions for Prayer

1. Perhaps using a prayer journal, reflect on a struggle you have had with one of your children. Would more freedom have shifted the dynamic?

2. If you have a child who currently questions or rejects Christian faith, take your concern to God in prayer. Envision all that is good in your child and give thanks for his or her presence in your life.

Discussion Questions

1. What do you think of Pope Francis's emphasis on freedom over control? Do some cultural contexts make this sort of parenting ethic more difficult?

2. What practices in your family or families you know seem to work to cultivate virtue, especially the virtue of solidarity? What could parishes do to better support parents in their efforts to cultivate virtue in their children?

8 The Tough Issues
Accompanying, Discerning, and Integrating Weakness

No one can be condemned for ever, because that is not the logic of the Gospel!
—AL 297

This chapter, more than any of the others, is primarily written for pastors. It includes some of the most technical passages of the document and some of the most hotly disputed footnotes! It is important for lay Catholics (especially those in what the document calls "irregular" unions) to read because Pope Francis is describing what their pastoral care ought to look like. He is also outlining a framework for personal discernment or reflecting on an individual situation and making decisions. Although the question of the possibility of divorced and remarried Catholics taking Communion received the most attention in the press coverage of the synod and AL, this chapter's significance is far broader. Francis draws on his earlier document, *Evangelii Gaudium*, in order to integrate the insights of contemporary moral theology into official Catholic teaching on family ethics.

While he connects to the final document of the synod, some work of Pope John Paul II's, and the International Theological

Commission, this chapter bears Francis's distinctive stamp. The image of the church as a "field hospital" (AL 291) that never fails to uphold the ideal, while accompanying the weak and wounded, and practicing mercy, is fundamental. As noted in chapter 6, this image was articulated in the interviews Pope Francis gave in the earliest days of his pontificate and it has been central to his preaching and teaching ever since. The church as field hospital concentrates on what is most essential: healing the brokenhearted, recognizing that God is working in everyone's lives, no matter what their situation. For pastors, the image is a call to change the way parishes operate. For laypeople, the image is an apology for past obtuseness, an assurance of mercy, and an invitation to return and be a source of mercy and healing for others. We'll explore the operations of the field hospital in five steps: gradualness, discernment, mitigating factors, rules, and mercy.

Gradualness

As we discussed in chapter 7, "gradualness" was the subject of a lot of debate at the synod. Some bishops at the synod drew on the term to make the point that couples that cohabit or live in civil marriage who may not be living up to the fullness of the church's ideal may nonetheless realize aspects of what the church hopes for in marriage (e.g., selfless love, generosity, responsibility, fidelity) and could possibly, with good pastoral care, grow in their capacity to live out the ideal. Some noted that John Paul II used the "law of gradualness" to describe stages of growth for those not capable of carrying out the moral law (AL 295). Other bishops worried that such language (previously used by theologians to argue for greater tolerance of Catholics who found themselves unable to live out Catholic teaching on masturbation, contraception, or same-sex marriage) would constitute a watering down of church teaching.

Francis indicates understanding of the worries of traditionalists, but sides with those who argued for retrieving the concept of "gradualness." He gives the example of a cohabiting couple, whose relationship may be marked by deep affection and responsibility for children (AL 293). Instead of alienating a couple like this, by describing their situation as "living in sin," Francis advocates leading with mercy, trying to understand social and cultural factors that may be influencing their decision to live together, entering into respectful dialogue with the couple, and encouraging openness to growth. He claims that it is possible for the church to welcome and encourage cohabiting couples while upholding the ideal of marriage, just as Jesus entered into dialogue with the Samaritan woman (John 4:1-26). If the church is to be an effective field hospital, it has to meet people where they are and figure out how best to help them.

Discernment

Once people are welcomed in the church as field hospital, the church's pastors need to figure out how to aid them in their own moral discernment. Francis makes a strong claim about the character of the church in the beginning of this section. The way of Jesus, and thus the way of the church, is not "casting off" but practicing mercy and welcoming people back (AL 296). This is who we are. No one is condemned forever. The mercy that Jesus offers, and thus that the church offers, is "unmerited, unconditional and gratuitous" (297). We do not deserve to be saved or forgiven, and yet we are. This doesn't mean that we aren't constantly called to conversion. But the church is rarely in the position of having to cut anyone off for good. It is almost always possible to offer mercy and to help people discern how they can do better.

> If the church is to be an effective field hospital, it has to meet people where they are and figure out how best to help them.

Note how often Francis emphasizes the diversity of people's situations. He references John Paul II's attempt to distinguish between those who leave and those who are abandoned, between those whose first marriages were valid and those who are subjectively certain of the invalidity of their first marriages.[1] Then he notes that, according to *Gaudium et Spes*, it is not always possible for a couple living in a second marriage, and unable to separate, to follow church teaching and "live as brother and sister" (n. 329). The key for Francis is that these are just a few of many possibilities. People's situations differ. This is why it is impossible to provide general rules that apply to everyone.

Rather, the pope encourages "responsible personal and pastoral discernment of particular cases," and gives criteria for good discernment: humility, discretion, love for church and its teaching, "a sincere search for God's will," and a desire to respond to God (AL 300). Recall that early in the document, Pope Francis made a bold statement about the church: it should guide consciences, not replace them (37). Here, he makes his claim more specific, saying discernment needs to be better integrated into church teaching (299). We can't just present the teaching as a set of rules, because that's not all there is to it.

This means that those in "irregular" situations are not to be ostracized: "They are baptized; they are brothers and sisters; the Holy Spirit pours into their hearts gifts and talents for the good of all" (299). We know from surveys that many feel ostracized, but the pope says they should instead feel welcome in the Christian community, and trusted to do their own moral discernment.

Mitigating Factors

In the church as field hospital, there is a recognition of mitigating factors or circumstances that make it tough to assess any one person's culpability for sin. Again, the pope is aware that some see this as watering down the tradition. But he claims such recognition is *part of* the Catholic moral tradition, so it "can no longer simply be said that all those in any 'irregular' situation are living in a state of mortal sin and are deprived of sanctifying grace" (AL 301).

Working with analogies shows the reasonableness of Francis's point. Moral theologian James Bretzke, SJ, gives the admittedly bizarre example of an actor who doesn't realize his gun (a prop) is loaded and accidentally kills a fellow actor.[2] Looking at the scene from the outside, it looks like murder. But once we understand motive (he intended to pretend to shoot the other actor), limited knowledge (he had no idea the gun was loaded), and context (a play), the action looks less like murder than accidental killing and the actor's culpability lessens considerably. It would just be wrong to say that the actor and someone who intentionally killed another person with forethought and malice engaged in the same action or were similarly guilty. Bretzke moves from this example to discuss the complex situations of gang members who sincerely believe in the morality of honor killings. One might also think about killing in self-defense, in just war, or out of mercy for the dying. Killing is always evil, but it is not always equally wrong, nor are all who kill equally morally culpable.

In various situations, people might know a rule but not understand its value, or their context might be such that every possible choice would be at least somewhat sinful, or they might have limited ability to make good decisions. Even the Catechism lists factors that can affect a person's ability to act (e.g., ignorance, duress, habit, fear). The Catholic tradition has always held that circumstances may lessen culpability (AL 302). Remembering this should keep everyone humble as we respect other people's decisions in conscience to act as they believe God is asking them to (303).

Note that Francis isn't questioning the existence of objective moral rules here, but he is saying that we've confused knowing the rules with assessing someone's sinfulness or culpability. In the Catholic tradition, we just can't do that without taking circumstances into account.

Rules

For those who looked to him to provide an answer to the contentious synod debates about Eucharist for the divorced and remarried, Francis provides an answer in this section, but it is not an answer that settles all debates. The "field hospital" spirit of the section is clear. Moral laws aren't "stones to throw at people's lives" (AL 305); mercy always comes first. We can't just ask whether someone's actions conform to a rule or law; this would be an insufficient way to discern that person's fidelity to God. With this set up, the pope seems to reopen a debate among moral theologians in the 1990s about the existence of "absolute moral norms." Most theologians agree that some absolute moral norms exist (e.g., murder, adultery, rape, torture), but most of the moral life involves situations that are far less clear (e.g., Does voting for candidate X constitute sinful involvement in moral evil for me if all possible candidates advocate or tolerate at least some actions the Catholic tradition calls morally evil?). Not to see the complexity is to succumb to a rule-based morality that is "superficial" and "reductive" (304, 305). Even Thomas Aquinas, the main source of Catholic thinking on natural law, indicated that only the most general moral norms apply to all, while the more particular we get, the more variety and change we should expect.[3] To fail to see people and situations in their complexity is to judge with a "closed heart," the pope says (AL 305), giving credence to those with more progressive views.

So what about that controversial footnote? It's number 351. It seems to indicate that, at least in some cases, divorced and remarried persons may, in consultation with their pastors, discern that they have confronted and confessed their responsibility for the failure of their first marriage and would be best served by a return to the sacraments. This has been called the "internal forum" solution. Francis repeats some of his own well-known phrases to support his judgment: the confessional is not to be a "torture chamber" and the Eucharist is not "a prize for the perfect." Following his own method, he does not roll out a new rule, but he does open a door and encourage pastors to move beyond black-and-white thinking in order to help divorced and remarried people find "ways of responding to God and growing in the midst of limits," instead of blocking that growth (305).

Now, some theologians were very worried about the possibility that Francis might open this door and some are even encouraging him to "clarify" the move he did make.[4] Debate even continues on whether he made a move or not. But wherever one comes down in these debates, Francis wants charity or love to be the mark of the church and he wants pastors and ordinary Christians to remember that sin and the possibility of atoning for sin are a fundamental part of our tradition (306). He wants that recognition to shape pastoral care.

Mercy

So much hangs on what one thinks of mercy as the center of Francis's thinking and acting. Some argue this focus fails to grapple with Jesus' challenging call to discipleship. Francis says no, the church isn't giving up on its teaching on lifelong marriage. The field hospital is not about "relativism" or "reticence" (AL 307).

We still need serious pastoral efforts to strengthen marriage and prevent marital breakdown.

But, and this is a crucial "but," mercy for Francis is not second to truth. It does not take anything away from truth. It is *part of* the truth. Francis is convinced that when the church walks with people in difficult situations, it is doing what Jesus taught, just as it is when it lifts up the ideal of indissoluble marriage. To see the goodness of the Spirit "in the midst of human weakness, . . . to treat the weak with compassion, . . . not to judge or condemn, . . . to enter into the reality of people's lives," to see the complexity—all of this is what Jesus commanded us to do (308).

> Francis is convinced that when the church walks with people in difficult situations, it is doing what Jesus taught, just as it is when it lifts up the ideal of indissoluble marriage.

After beginning the section with a strong foundation in documents from the synod, he ends by liberally quoting from *Evangelii Gaudium*, the papal bull with which he opened the Year of Mercy, and the gospel. Christians "show mercy because mercy was first shown to us," not because we earned it, but in spite of our inadequacy (AL 310). Some say we can't overemphasize mercy at the expense of truth or offer mercy to those who persist in sin. To do so, they claim, would not actually be merciful at all. However, to juxtapose mercy and truth, Francis says, is to water down the gospel, because "mercy is the fullness of justice and the most radiant manifestation of God's truth" (311).

The section ends not with a rule but with a hope: that faithful Christians will go to their pastors with confidence expecting welcome, challenge, and hope; and that pastors will respond with sensitivity, a desire to understand, and mercy (312). As long as we all know we're in the field hospital together, as long as we see the places of gradualness, discernment, mitigating factors, rules, and mercy, this pope is willing to leave the local churches to work out the details.

Suggestions for Prayer

1. As you think about Pope Francis's warnings about rule-based, black-and-white thinking, reflect on situations in your own life in which you might have erred on the side of judgment instead of mercy.
2. Are there situations in your own life in which you may have been too hard or too easy on yourself? Meditate on one of those decisions and reflect on whether you might need to forgive yourself or challenge yourself.

Discussion Questions

1. The pope tries very hard to argue that we can teach the truth about marriage while respecting the complexity of people's lives. Do you worry that most people will see this section of the document as a watering down of Catholic teaching, despite the pope's best intentions? Does the complexity the pope claims as part of the Catholic moral tradition seem new or is this the way you have been taught?
2. What more could local parishes do to make divorced and remarried people feel welcome? Is allowing for reception of the Eucharist essential?

Conclusion

Why Get Married?
Why Stay Married?
A Spirituality for Marriage and Family

The two are thus mutual reflections of that divine love which comforts with a word, a look, a helping hand, a caress, an embrace. For this reason "to want to form a family is to resolve to be a part of God's dream . . . of building a world where no one will feel alone."
—AL 321

    In his conclusion, Pope Francis returns to speaking directly to married couples. He wants to express complex theological claims about the sacrament of marriage in down-to-earth terms that resonate with people's experience of the profound depth of married life. In Pope John Paul II's *Familiaris Consortio*, the concluding section on the task of the family as domestic church sticks much more closely to traditional sacramental language and religious practices. In contrast, Pope Francis offers a spirituality that expresses the essence of Catholic sacramental theology in everyday language. In doing so, he also underlines once again the promise and potential of marriage in light of the five themes that animate his document as a whole. There is no back story here. All the attention is on married people and the joy of love.

1. *Intimacy and passion are good in themselves and worth cultivating for life.* We have heard a lot about the goodness of married love and the need to cultivate it throughout AL, but especially in chapters 2 and 4. Notice how in the conclusion, the spirituality of love is brought forward. A reader might ask, "What does it mean to say that God is with us or that grace sustains us?" Francis answers that when people are fully themselves, authentic, alive, and loving, that is where God dwells (AL 315). When people live together, they have to sacrifice. Christians see that sacrifice as a part of sanctification or growth in holiness that leads to deeper union with God. But the togetherness itself is also essential, because human beings are fundamentally social, and because we know God in loving and being loved. So when we live together in communion, God dwells with us.

   Historically the Christian tradition had a hard time seeing marriage as a true path to God compared with vowed celibacy. Francis affirms marriage as a path to "mystical union" with God (316). Marriage is a joy because it is "the experience of belonging completely to another person," but it is also a challenge, a commitment reaffirmed each day, to be "for the other a sign and instrument of the closeness of the Lord, who never abandons us" (319). It is a passionate love that must be cultivated, and thus a way to enter more deeply into union with the God who is love.

2. *Christians accompany people who experience brokenness or failure in marriage.* Yet, Francis does not present an unattainable spirituality. Though he makes reference to family

prayer and other practices of popular piety (318), he emphasizes that no family is perfect (325). Once we really take this in, we know that no one has attained "good Catholic family" status once and for all. All families need constant growth. There is no pure love this side of heaven. This caution about high expectations also leads Francis to warning that there is no justification for judging those whose marriages or families break apart. No matter what happens, we are called not to divide the perfect from the imperfect, within a family or outside of it, but to accompany or "keep walking together" (325).

3. *Social forces make marriage difficult to sustain.* Though specific social forces are not named, notice the poignant reference to "[m]oments of pain and difficulty" and "the darkest hours of a family's life" (317). We can insert here experiences of a parent being sent to prison or having to go to a foreign country to find work, the loss of a child to gang violence, or long-term unemployment. Francis tries to explain how reflecting on the cross can shed light on experiences of suffering and transform them (317). This spiritual lens for viewing suffering does not negate the responsibility to work to change unjust social structures, but it does give families another way to see and respond to the social forces that make their lives so difficult.

4. *Married life is imperfect.* Francis does not present couples with a spirituality for the perfect. Every time he identifies an ideal, he remembers to keep it real. So, we are to contemplate our loved ones and see Christ in them, especially when their limitations are clearly on display (323). Family gives us the chance to share in God's creative work, God's love, even God's dream, but "each person is for the other a constant challenge from the Holy Spirit" (321). In

marriage there is an "experience of belonging completely to another person" (319), but we need to grow into a "spiritual realism" that allows us to see that only God can fully satisfy (320). Even the greatest earthly love is revelatory and sacramental, but not perfect. Spiritualities of marriage and family claiming more than this go too far. What Francis offers is beauty with plenty of weeds.

5. *Love is fruitful.* Finally, the spirituality Francis presents is not for an insular love of two (even two and their children). The idea of overflowing love returns here, as Francis claims that a Christian family becomes more itself by "going forth" and sharing its love with the world, in hospitality and service to others (324). It's not that a Christian family adds service projects to the mix of love that characterizes other marriages. But rather that in its common life, it is also at the same time "a vital cell for transforming the world." And in this work they are "[l]ed by the Spirit" (324).

At the close of this, the longest papal document ever written, Francis leaves us with his best effort to describe how God is present in our families, in times of joy and suffering, in the midst of injustice and imperfection, when we attend to each other and when we open our hearts and homes to others, and when we accompany each other. The grace that is present in Catholic marriage is not a magic remedy that solves all problems. Marriage remains an earthly reality and as long as human beings are imperfect, there will be misunderstanding, pain, and loneliness among those who have pledged to love each other. We are but imperfect channels of God's love. Yet the possibilities present in the Catholic vision of marriage are real. Whatever the outcome of ongoing debates among theologians, if couples read The Joy of Love and are inspired to embrace the daring adventure of marriage, the long process that brought it about will have been worthwhile.

Notes

Introduction

1. Joshua J. McElwee, "Vatican Asks for Parish-Level Input on Synod Document," *National Catholic Reporter*, October 31, 2013, https://www.ncronline.org/news/vatican/vatican-asks-parish-level-input-synod-document. Links to the survey and accompanying letter from the Vatican are included.

2. Ibid.

3. Many synod-related documents, including the *Relatio Synodi* or final reports from 2014 and 2015, are available at http://www.usccb.org/issues-and-action/marriage-and-family/2014-2015-synods-of-bishops-on-the-family.cfm. The 2014 midterm report is available at http://en.radiovaticana.va/news/2014/10/13/synod_on_family_midterm_report_presented,_2015_synod_announ/1108442.

4. Antonio Spadaro, "A Big Heart Open to God," *America*, September 30, 2013, http://americamagazine.org/pope-interview.

5. Available at http://www.usccb.org/issues-and-action/marriage-and-family/2014-2015-synods-of-bishops-on-the-family.cfm.

6. John Paul II, *Familiaris Consortio* (1981), https://w2.vatican.va/content/john-paul-ii/en/apost_exhortations/documents/hf_jp-ii_exh_19811122_familiaris-consortio.html.

7. See, e.g., Andrew J. Cherlin, *The Marriage-Go-Round: The State of Marriage and the Family in America Today* (New York: Vintage, 2010); and Robert D. Putnam, *Our Kids: The American Dream in Crisis* (New York: Simon and Schuster, 2015).

8. Francis, *Laudato Sì*, 2015, http://w2.vatican.va/content/francesco/en/encyclicals/documents/papa-francesco_20150524_enciclica-laudato-si.html.

Chapter 1

1. John Paul II, *Familiaris Consortio* (1981) 28.

2. Paul VI, *Gaudium et Spes* (1965) 52.

3. See, e.g., Halvor Moxnes, *Putting Jesus in His Place: A Radical Vision of Household and Kingdom* (Louisville: Westminster John Knox, 2003).

4. These include Mark 3:31-35; Luke 14:26; and Mark 10:29-30.

5. See, e.g., Elisabeth Schüssler Fiorenza, *In Memory of Her: A Feminist Theological Reconstruction of Christian Origins* (New York: Crossroads, 1994).

Chapter 2

1. National Marriage Project, *The State of Our Unions* (2010), http://nationalmarriageproject.org/wp-content/uploads/2012/06/Union_11_12_10.pdf.

2. Note the development in Catholic teaching between Pius XI's encyclical *Casti Connubii* (1931), in which the pope decried feminist movements and called for a proper "order of love" in the home, including wifely submission, and John Paul II's Letter to Women (1995), which celebrated women's roles in the world and advocated spousal equality.

Chapter 3

1. Richard Gaillardetz, *A Daring Promise: A Spirituality of Christian Marriage* (Liguori, MO: Liguori, 2007).

Chapter 4

1. Stanley Hauerwas explained his well-known comment in an interview in *U.S. Catholic* 56.6 (June 1991): 6–13.

2. Martin Luther King Jr., "Loving Your Enemies," in *Strength to Love* (Philadelphia: Fortress, 1981), 49–57.

3. Other references to violence appear in paragraphs 19, 20, 45, 51, 53, and 153. Previous popes have made similarly strong statements about contraception but Francis, while repeating the church's teaching on birth control, makes no such claim. Violence receives his harshest condemnation.

4. WHO, *Global and Regional Estimates of Violence against Women*, 2, 17, http://www.who.int/reproductivehealth/publications/violence/9789241564625/en/.

Chapter 5

1. Edward Pentin, "Catholic Scholars Appeal to Pope Francis to Repudiate 'Errors' in *Amoris Laetitia*," *National Catholic Register*, July 11, 2016, http://www.ncregister.com/blog/edward-pentin/catholic-scholars-appeal-to-pope-francis-to-repudiate-errors-in-amoris-laet/#ixzz4E8hCcMge.

Chapter 6

1. See Antonio Spadaro, "A Big Heart Open to God," *America*, September 30, 2013, http://americamagazine.org/pope-interview.

2. Francis, *Evangelii Gaudium* (2013) 169–73, http://w2.vatican.va/content/francesco/en/apost_exhortations/documents/papa-francesco_esortazione-ap_20131124_evangelii-gaudium.html.

3. "Updated: Most Marriages Today Are Invalid, Pope Francis Suggests," *Catholic News Agency*, June 16, 2016, http://www.catholicnewsagency.com/news/most-marriages-today-are-invalid-pope-francis-suggests-51752/. The pope revised his initial comments to say that "a portion" of marriages are invalid rather than "a great majority."

4. Richard Gaillardetz, *A Daring Promise: A Spirituality of Christian Marriage* (Liguori, MO: Liguori, 2007), 50.

5. "Pope: Divorced and Remarried People Not Excommunicated," *Vatican Radio*, May 8, 2015, http://en.radiovaticana.va/news/2015/08/05/pope_divorced_and_remarried_people_not_excommunicated/1163121.

6. Jason Adkins et al., "Finding Hope in the Church's 'Hard Teachings' on Marriage and Communion," *America*, November 12, 2015, http://americamagazine.org/issue/remember-our-children.

7. Rachel Donadio, "On Gay Priests, Pope Francis Asks, 'Who Am I to Judge?,'" *New York Times*, July 29, 2013, http://www.nytimes.com/2013/07/30/world/europe/pope-francis-gay-priests.html.

Chapter 7

1. See, e.g., David Cloutier, "Gradualism and Holiness," *Commonweal*, October 13, 2014, https://www.commonwealmagazine.org/blog/gradualism-and-holiness-0.

Chapter 8

1. John Paul II, *Familiaris Consortio* (1981) 83–84.

2. James T. Bretzke, *A Morally Complex World: Engaging Contemporary Moral Theology* (Collegeville, MN: Liturgical Press, 2004), 73–74.

3. Thomas Aquinas, *Summa Theologica* I–II, q. 94, a. 4. Francis also cites the International Theological Commission to support his argument on the importance of considering circumstances: "In Search of a Universal Ethic: A New Look at the Natural Law," http://www.vatican.va/roman_curia/congregations/cfaith/cti_documents/rc_con_cfaith_doc_20090520_legge-naturale_en.html.

4. Joshua J. McElwee, "Signers of Document Critiquing 'Amoris Laetitia' Revealed," *National Catholic Reporter*, July 22, 2016, https://www.ncronline.org/news/vatican/signers-document-critiquing-amoris-laetitia-revealed.

For Further Reading

Bennett, Jana Marguerite. *Water is Thicker than Blood: An Augustinian Theology of Marriage and Singleness.* New York: Oxford University Press, 2008.

Cahill, Lisa Sowle. *Family: A Christian Social Perspective.* Minneapolis: Fortress, 2000.

Farley, Margaret. *Just Love: A Framework for Christian Sexual Ethics.* New York: Continuum, 2006.

Gaillardetz, Richard. *A Daring Promise: A Spirituality of Christian Marriage.* Rev. ed. Liguori, MO: Liguori, 2007.

Grabowski, John S. *Sex and Virtue: An Introduction to Sexual Ethics.* Washington, DC: Catholic University of America Press, 2003.

Lasnoski, Kent J. *Vocation to Virtue: Christian Marriage as a Consecrated Life.* Washington, DC: Catholic University of America Press, 2014.

McCarthy, David Matzko. *Sex and Love in the Home.* New ed. London: SCM Press, 2004.

Reimer-Barry, Emily. *Catholic Theology of Marriage in the Era of HIV and AIDS: Marriage for Life.* Lanham, MD: Lexington, 2015.

Roche, Mary Doyle. *Children, Consumerism, and the Common Good.* Lanham, MD: Lexington, 2009.

Rubio, Julie Hanlon. *Family Ethics: Practices for Christians.* Washington, DC: Georgetown University Press, 2010.